When God heals,
He does not take the healing back.

Ask and You Shall Receive:

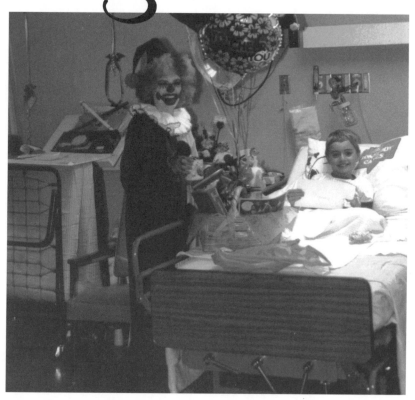

A Miracle for Steven

Karen Vincent Zizzo

Enlighten Publishing
"Waking up to what already is present."
Ancaster, Ontario, Canada

Enlighten Publishing,
27 Legend Court, P.O. Box 10114,
Ancaster, Ontario
Canada
L9K 1P3
1-800-538-5194
www.enlightenpublishing.com

Library and Archives Canada Cataloguing in Publication

Zizzo, Karen Vincent, 1953-
Ask and you shall receive : a miracle for Steven / authored by Karen Vincent Zizzo.

ISBN 0-9736696-0-8

1. Zizzo, Steven--Health. 2. Neuroblastoma--Patients--Biography.
3. Zizzo family. 4. Spiritual healing. I. Title.

BT732.5.Z59 2004   362.198'929948'0092   C2004-906264-6

First edition

Cover Photo by Steven Vincent Zizzo, Tamarama Beach, New South Wales, Australia
Cover Illustration by Willem Pretorius
Cover Design by Rose Gowsell

Book Design and Layout by Craig A. Bondy of Byond Communication
Prepared for publication by Solotext Editorial www.solotext.com

I dedicate this book
to all of those who want to believe in
The Power of Prayer.

May this story give you the Hope and the Faith to believe that prayer is a powerful force, and that God is there for all of us.

"Ask and you shall receive."
You don't always receive what you ask for;
the gift may be in recognizing "what" you receive.
Anyone can ask.
God is the God of the impossible.
Miracles do happen.

iracle:

...an extraordinary and welcome event
that is not explicable by natural or scientific laws,
attributed to a divine agency.

According to the Concise Oxford Dictionary, 10th Edition, Oxford University Press.

Contents

Foreword

Preface

Acknowledgements

Foreword

I am a true believer that we meet the right people at the right time to get the things done that God feels need to be done. I met Karen Zizzo at a business meeting. The subject of the meeting was not powerful in either of our minds, but we had come to the meeting because someone else thought that we should meet. We both had this overwhelming feeling that we should be there and had even reorganized our schedules so that we could attend. As it turned out, we were not there to talk about the business, but we did need to meet.

I looked across the table and asked Karen, "What do you feel passionately about?" She replied, "I have a book I need to publish." Without hesitation I said, "I can help you with that." I had just completed three years of research to find a publisher and learned about getting my own book published. I had the answers she needed.

A few days earlier, Karen had asked God for His help. She had prayed, "Dear Lord, I need Your help. I want to get this book finished and published, but I need an editor and a publisher that can help me get the finished product. If it is Your will to have this book finished too, please send me that help." Forty-eight hours later we were sitting at the table across from each other and I had asked the right question. This book, *Ask and You Shall Receive: A Miracle for Steven,* was completed because of her prayer.

I truly believe that those who read this book will be given strength in their own lives. After reading about the situation that shook the Zizzo family to their very foundations, people will be inspired. It will amaze many how an unflinching belief in the power of prayer and an all-consuming love brought them though this frightening period. Regardless of what you face in life–

obstacles, challenges, disappointments, or emotional and physical pain—you will have insight into the power of prayer, and the power of the outpouring of love and concern from everyone around you.

In the pages of this book, Karen and her family have courageously shared their story. They have returned to the past and dredged up all of the emotions and realities of that painful period in their lives so that through their words, through this book, they can help others. I encourage you to read it with an open mind and heart. I am extremely proud to have been a part of the project. Like everyone who reads it, I have been given renewed faith, greater hope, and a strength that comes from believing again in the power of prayer.

Judy Suke
President, Triangle Seminars
Professional Speaker, Entertainer and Author
Distinguished Toastmaster
Member of the National Speaker's Association
Waterdown, Ontario, Canada

Preface

*ears of experience,
plus knowledge,
plus reflection,
equals WISDOM*

The experience within these pages happened in 1987 …it is now 2004.

I have to begin by explaining the two main reasons why it took me so long to write this book.

Number One: I needed years of reflection to share exactly what happened. It is said that years of experience, plus knowledge, plus reflection, equals wisdom. Hopefully, I have acquired some wisdom over the years. I feel I have.

Number Two: Throughout the years, there were times that I was asked to put our experience to paper. I could not write the story while Steven, our oldest son, was young and still growing up. I did not want him to be adversely affected by people seeking him out as "the miracle boy." I wanted his youth to be as normal as possible.

He is now twenty-five years old and in medical school in Australia. He understands that something powerful happened and even has encouraged me to tell the story. He realizes that it may help others and give them hope.

Some real soul-searching had to be done as to whether our family should share this very personal account of Steven's serious medical ordeal. Our final decision was based on a need to show our gratitude, and our heartfelt desire to give hope to others.

As we began to share our story, many people asked us why we allowed such an invasion of our family's privacy. They also warned that people would be skeptical of our story. Was it a misdiagnosis? Or, was it a miracle—a miracle resulting from divine intervention created by the power of prayer?

You will see, as events unfold in the story, that something was happening that could not be explained. Our family experienced the loving and focused power of prayer, and we are eternally grateful. It was through the Scripture, "Ask, and ye shall receive, that your joy may be full" [John 16:24] that we were guided to trust in a positive outcome. Making our public request for prayer ensured that the power was spread over many people earnestly focusing their thoughts and energy on our son Steven, and on all of us as a family. God is the God of the impossible and He enlightened many to the powerful force of prayer during that time.

Even though we sometimes felt like saying "No" when invited to tell our story, something inside us wouldn't let us do that. Something miraculous happened and it is almost as though that unbelievable time in our lives must be shared. We even feel a responsibility to tell others.

My husband, Richard, and I both agree that telling this story blesses us over and over again. As you are reading this, we are similarly blessed. Others tell us that they also feel blessed in hearing the story.

It is our desire to share this story with the intention of bringing you closer to experiencing your own Hope, Faith, Trust, and Love in God. May this story give you the Hope and the Faith to believe that prayer is a powerful force, and that God is there for all of us.

Acknowledgements

I want to say a heartfelt thank you to those who have contributed to make this book possible.

To my husband, Richard, whose inspiration, unconditional support, and love motivated me to reach for my dream of finishing this book. I thank you for your generosity of spirit, collaborating with me, and allowing me to candidly tell our personal story.

To my children, Steven, Laura, and Ryan, for your constant inspiration, support, and understanding. Thank you for being who you are. You always encouraged me and pushed me to finish the book. You would say, "Just do it." I want you to know how proud I am of all of you and your accomplishments, and that I love you dearly.

To my loving extended family, who encouraged me, and cheered me on. Thank you to all of you. You were so much a part of this story. Your love, support, and prayers were a constant, and always are. I want you to know how much you are appreciated and loved.

To the many friends, who made suggestions, offered prayers, and shared stories, I thank you for your encouragement. I truly value our friendship.

To my gifted manuscript developer, Judy Suke, who helped me focus, commit to regular times to work, and get this book finished. Thank you for your personal commitment to my project. "Focus and finish," were words I needed to hear. You made the writing process fun.

To Manisha Solomon, of Solotext Editorial, thank you for your candid suggestions and for your competent organizational skills in completing this project. Your knowledge and connections were invaluable.

To Sharon Buzelli, thank you for helping me get the first draft together. Every journey begins with the first step.

I especially offer up a thank you to God for the loving kindness and steadfast blessings that I am continually grateful for. It is for the glory of Him that I felt compelled to share this story. We placed our trust in the palm of His hand. This is a story of Faith, Hope, and Love.

ur Story

CHAPTER ONE

The Nightmare Begins

"Dad, you hurt my neck!"

It was January 1987. Our eldest son, Steven, was seven years old. In the normal fashion of a seven-year-old, he was quite rambunctious. Hockey was his favourite sport. My husband, Richard, was helping remove Steven's equipment after the Saturday morning game when Steven cringed, rubbed the right side of his neck under his ear, and exclaimed, "Dad, you hurt my neck!" Little did we know how those five words would impact the rest of our lives.

Richard observed a lump on Steven's neck and made a mental note, "OK, he's got a lump on his neck about the size of a nickel." Richard then responded to Steven, "No problem, Steven." Being a physician, Richard knew that lumps could be trouble. Steven recoiled and repeated, "No, you really hurt it!"

◊ ◊ ◊

It happened to be a very busy Saturday. We were having a party for my mother. She was celebrating her sixtieth birthday, or as we referred to it–"her twenty-ninth birthday for the thirty-first time." Over the course of the day, Richard continued to watch the lump on Steven's neck grow bigger. By early evening, the lump was clearly visible to us all; it was the size of a small orange. The lump was both tender and somewhat painful. The skin colour looked normal and Steven had no fever. "I think Steven's got early mononucleosis. It's atypical," Richard said. "He's looking well, but I still have questions." I knew that "atypical" meant that this was not a normal presentation.

In fact, Steven looked absolutely fine. He had always been a normal, healthy, and athletic child, so we were trying really hard not to overreact. However, we could not help but be concerned. The lump had become so noticeable that people at the party asked about it. In order to keep the focus on the birthday celebration, Richard casually responded, "I don't know. He probably bruised himself playing hockey. But, we will keep an eye on it."

Richard monitored the lump all day Sunday. By Sunday night, he was very worried. The lump had not gone down. All doctors worry about overreacting or underreacting to ailments that strike their own families so they try to avoid diagnosing them.

"Karen," Richard said to me once Steven had been put to bed, "I would like to share the responsibility. I don't want to diagnose my own child. Call our family doctor and get him to take a peak at this thing and get his opinion."

On Monday, I was able to arrange an appointment for Steven to see our family doctor for that afternoon. After a quick but thorough examination, our doctor agreed with Richard's initial diagnosis. It was likely to be "an atypical presentation of a virus, such as mononucleosis." With mononucleosis, people usually feel tired and are easily fatigued. They have a sore throat and a rash. They also have swollen glands on either side of their neck.

With a swelling on only one side, our doctor feared that it could be something more obscure. He ordered a chest X-ray and blood work to be done as soon as possible. Steven and I went across the street to the medical lab to get these tests done. I was not expecting anything else than a possible case of mononucleosis—certainly not what was to follow. Because we were just following the orders of our doctor, Steven and I did not think much of these tests. It was Richard who had a sense of uneasiness. I just did not want to go there, yet; I did not want to cross the bridge before we came to it.

By the time we got home from the lab, it was dinner time. I thanked the baby sitter and she left for the day. Steven went into the family room and turned on the television while I prepared dinner. Laura, our five-year-old, ran up to show me a picture that she had drawn that day while she was at school. Ryan, our two-year-old, brought me his chosen toy and wanted me to play with him. The events of the afternoon soon became shadowed by the usual dinner-hour activities. Richard and I will never forget what happened only a few hours later.

◊ ◊ ◊

Although it was important for us to eat dinner as a family on a daily basis, Richard was later than usual that evening and did not arrive home until about 7:00 p.m. I was already upstairs getting our three children ready for bed. Richard was eating his dinner in the kitchen, a sausage-on-a-bun, when the phone rang. I called out for Richard to pick up the phone. Between bathing one child, chasing another with pyjama bottoms, and diapering a third, there was no way that I could get to the phone in time.

"Hi, how are you doing?" I heard Richard say to the caller. After a few pleasantries back and forth, Richard silenced. It was our family doctor. Richard later told me that he, at first, thought that the family doctor was calling as a professional courtesy to tell us that everything was alright. When the doctor got down to business, Richard realized differently.

The doctor told Richard that the radiologist had just called. Being a doctor, Richard knew that the radiologist would not call the family doctor immediately with the results if they were good. "That doesn't sound good. What's going on?" Richard asked. The doctor wanted Steven to see a specialist the next day to "check things out further."

"What for?" Richard asked. He was told that the radiologist had found a spot on Steven's lung.

"Tell me about the spot on his lung," I heard Richard say.

"He has something on the left side," was all that the doctor offered, which Richard later relayed to me.

"Tell me what he has on the left side of his lung!" Richard said to him in a firm voice. The doctor seemed to be purposely dragging out the conversation to ease the blow of the news. Finally, he told Richard that the radiologist saw something in the lung field.

From where I was, I could tell that Richard was frustrated. "I'm a doctor! Tell me what you're talking about!" The doctor's next words were those we would never forget: "He has a spot on the left lung…and they don't know what it is."

Richard, wanting the details of exactly what his little boy might have wrong, started firing off questions: "Where is it? Anterior? Posterior? Superior? Inferior? What's going on? Tell me what's going on here!"

The doctor told Richard that it looked "like a solid tumour."

"How big?" Richard asked. By this time, the conversation had totally distracted me from what I was doing. I stood as still as I could so I would not miss anything that was said by Richard.

"They had no trouble seeing it, Rick," was what Richard remembered the doctor to have said next. "You know, this is frustrating me! How big is it?" Richard said, completely irritated by this time.

"Seven centimetres!" was the next thing I heard Richard say. "In diameter? Centimetres? You must mean millimetres! Seven centimetres is huge! This is only a seven-year-old boy we're talking about! His chest isn't much bigger than that!"

The doctor reiterated that the radiologist had confirmed that it was seven centimetres.

Richard was told that there was a problem and that the doctors needed to deal with it.

"What are you suggesting we do?" Richard asked, trying to be calm and objective.

Again, he was told that Steven had to see the specialist immediately. Richard and our doctor spent a few more minutes discussing a plan for the next day.

I had to know what was going on. I sped through the bedtime rituals and stood at the top of the stairs. The parts of the conversation that I could hear pulled me downstairs. By the serious tone of Richard's voice during the phone conservation, I knew that something was amiss. I heard Richard hang up the phone, and then I heard nothing. It was so quiet that I thought he had left the room, but I had not heard his footsteps. I entered the kitchen to find Richard hunched in his chair, with his half-eaten dinner on the table. Upon lifting his head to see me enter the room, he let out the breath he had been holding. Then he inhaled a deep breath and just cried. Although I knew the conversation he had with the doctor was serious, I could not fathom what he had heard to elicit a reaction of this kind. I could only implore him to tell me what had happened.

Choking back tears, he haltingly relayed the conversation. I was listening, but my heart and my mind did not fully comprehend the extent of our problem. Realizing that I was not grasping what I was being told, and perhaps to clarify the situation for both of us, he continued, "This is really a bad thing: to have a tumour in your chest and a lump on the side of your neck. This means that a cancer has probably spread."

In an instant, I felt a tingle shoot through my body. I was hit with a spell of dizziness: my legs felt weak. I was suddenly so aware of my body and what was happening to it. I heard a gasp escape from my mouth. I had to leave. I wanted to run away from what I had just been told. I turned on my heel and left the room. I could not hold back the tears. As I left the kitchen, I suddenly felt overwhelmingly ill, like someone had just punched me in the stomach. I ran to the bathroom with all the speed my weighted legs could give me, grabbed the handle of the door to throw it open, and bent over the toilet just in time to vomit. I was retching in reaction to the emotional turmoil created by the shock of the situation. "This cannot be happening," I repeated to myself. In one moment, just like that, our lives were turned upside down.

While I stood in disbelief in the bathroom, looking at my reddened face in the mirror and brushing my dampened hair away from my eyes, and Richard sat in the same kitchen chair he was in before the call from the doctor, as if held there by some unseen force, the phone rang a second time. Richard stood up, walked over, and answered it. This time it was our parish priest. "Richard, this is Father Con. How are you? I am calling about Steven's upcoming First Holy Communion." Never has our priest called our home. Ever.

◊ ◊ ◊

Richard was so overcome by the power of the moment that tears welled up in his eyes, and he was unable to respond to Father Con's question.

"What's wrong, Richard?" Father Con asked.

"Just bear with me, Father," Richard said after clearing his throat. "I'll get it out, but it's going to take a few minutes...we have received some bad news." Richard told Father Con about the recent telephone conversation with our family doctor and explained Steven's medical problem. Richard relayed that the situation did not look good and ended the conversation by asking Father Con for prayers.

Our Story

We were unaware of the significance of Father Con's call at that point in time. Richard later questioned me: "Was it a coincidence? Did Father Con, in some way, learn of our situation?" We also did not realize that Richard's request to Father Con was just the beginning of our request for prayers. It would not be until days later that we would realize the powerful part that prayer would play in our lives.

◊ ◊ ◊

That evening, Richard telephoned his older brother, Angelo, who also is a physician. Angelo immediately came over to our house to discuss the seriousness of our situation. He tried to comfort us, to give us hope. "Don't forget, they could be wrong. They could be wrong! One, or even both of the tumours could be benign! These tumours may not even be related."

Richard and his brother knew that if both tumours were related and malignant, it would be Steven's death sentence. We all agreed that we desperately needed some hope.

We learned through this experience that you must never take a person's hope away. Ever. You cannot do that to people.

CHAPTER TWO

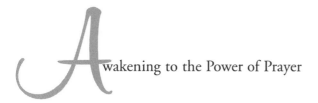wakening to the Power of Prayer

On Tuesday, when we told Steven that he would be going to a specialist's appointment instead of school, we chose to tell him in the simplest way possible: that he needed to see a paediatric specialist to determine what the lump in his neck was all about. For this appointment, Richard accompanied Steven and me. Our family doctor referred us to a pediatrician, a colleague of Richard's, whose office was located across the street from the hospital with which Richard was affiliated.

As a result of leaving our car in the hospital parking garage, we had to walk through the hospital to get to Steven's appointment. Along the way, we ran into a well-respected pediatric surgeon who Richard thought Steven would likely have to see at some point in the future. Richard and I smiled and exchanged pleasantries with the surgeon and then we went to Steven's appointment.

After examining Steven, the X-rays, and the information given to him, the pediatric oncologist told us that he wanted to talk to us in the hall. I turned to Steven and told him that we would be in the hall, talking to the doctor. "Play with the toys, Steven. We are just outside the door if you need us."

The pediatric oncologist confirmed that Steven had a tumour in his neck and a tumour in his chest. Now he had to determine a diagnosis, and Steven had to be admitted to the hospital right away.

The oncologist painted a bleak picture; he made us feel that we might as well buy the coffin. Both Richard and I felt as though he took away all hope. It was at this time that the gravity of the situation began to hit. Richard called his mother, and I called mine. We told them of the seriousness of the situation and asked them to call the rest of the family to let them know. I asked my mother to go to the house to relieve the babysitter, who had been with Laura and Ryan longer than anyone had anticipated.

Because the hospital across the street from the specialist's office did not specialize in children's medicine, Steven was transferred out of that hospital system and admitted into one that specialized in pediatric oncology. We did not end up seeing the well-respected pediatric surgeon who Richard thought would be responsible for Steven. Unbeknownst to us at the time but revealed after our ordeal, this man, like us, had a deep faith in the power of prayer.

◊ ◊ ◊

Normally, going to the hospital was not a novel event for Steven. He often accompanied his dad on a Saturday or Sunday, after hockey practice. He loved that the nurses would sneak a cookie and chocolate milk to him while his father did his rounds. On this day and at this unfamiliar hospital, however, there would be no milk and cookies for Steven.

A biopsy of the neck tumour, along with a bone biopsy, was arranged for that very evening. This was seen as an urgent matter. If the biopsy results were bad, then a Hickman catheter would be inserted into Steven's chest. This tube would establish a pathway directly into a large blood vessel attached to the heart so that medication could be administered without constantly using a needle. This was a regular procedure done for children so that they would not feel and look like a pincushion.

The doctors explained that they believed that Steven had a neuroblastoma. Neuroblastoma, which are generally found in children, are tumours that are highly malignant. They usually are found in the chest and originate in the adrenal glands or nervous system. It is an aggressive metastatic disease that goes from one spot to another. In a newborn, there is a chance of survival. If the child is four to six years old, a neuroblastoma is a much more serious problem: the chance of survival is much slimmer. Being a seven-year-old boy, and since the tumour appeared to have spread, we were told that Steven had no chance of survival. We were told that Steven would be "dead in three months."

"You have to entertain the possibility that both tumours are benign and unrelated or at least that one is benign," Richard said after we were given the grim and shocking prognosis.

The oncologist responded, "If I ever said that on an exam, I would fail the exam."

"If you did *not* say that on your exam, you *should* fail." Richard retorted. "You've got to say that there's a chance. You have to give me odds. You have to at least say that there's a chance that these tumours are not related." It was a different way of looking at the same thing, and Richard had to twist the doctor's arm to get the odds that the two tumours were not related.

"I'll give you one in a hundred," The oncologist said, grudgingly.

"I'll take it. I want something. You can even give me one in a thousand," Richard said after pondering the odds for a moment.

The pediatric oncologist, however, was totally negative. He was willing to give us the odds we wanted, but he believed it was all an exercise in futility. In his opinion, there was no hope. He did not even want to entertain the possibility of hope.

"You know, there is always a chance…," Richard repeated, trying to stay positive.

◊ ◊ ◊

We learned through this experience that you must never take

away a person's hope. Ever. You cannot do that to people.

The clinical diagnosis, and the way in which it was presented to us, could have taken away all shreds of our hope. We realized that no one had the right to take it away. There is always hope. There is always a chance that things are not as they appear. There are mistakes, there are miracles, and there is the power of prayer. No one person can accurately determine the outcome. You truly need to hold on to your faith and your hope, and you must trust in the power of your own belief in something beyond this world. It was this "something" that profoundly affected our family and showed many others that miracles do happen.

◊ ◊ ◊

After the appointment, Richard and I were emotionally numb. How could this be happening? The doctors involved with our case seemed to struggle with the best way to tell us about Steven's apparently hopeless situation. Some of them were bluntly "doom and gloom"; some of them tried to be sceptically positive. The bottom line was that they all said he was going to die. It was as simple as that: he was going to die. It was just a matter of when. It was a consensus among them that even receiving chemotherapy treatments at this point was not going to help. We were devastated. Yet, we realized that we had to hold on to a semblance of hope; otherwise, we would cave in and lose our strength to deal with what was ahead.

Steven's pediatric surgeon suggested a de-bulking, a reduction, of the primary tumour in Steven's chest. It was the size of a grape-fruit and was taking up the majority of our seven-year-old child's chest. The seriousness of the size of the tumour and the danger to the surrounding vital organs during surgery was frightening to us. Because of the nearness of the tumour to Steven's heart, we were told that if the aorta was nicked during surgery, he could die. We were also told that if the tumour was attached to the spine, its removal could make him a paraplegic. It was becoming apparent to us that the science of medicine was not going to be enough.

We told Steven that he was a seven-year-old child with a disease. What this situation really meant was that there was a war to fight. We said to him, "You know about wars, right?" We encouraged him to imagine the enemy. We explained that when there is a war, one country has to fight another country; there are good guys and there are bad guys, and they fight each other. We were attempting to explain the situation in terms that a seven-year-old could comprehend. "In order to win the war, battles must be fought. You have these little battles, and one of the battles is called a biopsy of your neck. Another battle is called getting the Hickman catheter connected to your heart. You have to fight all of these battles, and you have to win them. If you win most of them, you are going to win the war. So we are going to take one battle at a time." He thought that was cool.

This situation was proving to be a bigger battle than our family could handle alone. Richard and I both realized that we had to pray. As if we knew what the other was thinking, we immediately said to each other, "We will have to pray, really pray." We believed that it was the only thing that could help Steven now.

◊ ◊ ◊

I have always believed that God is the God of the impossible and that He actually hears prayers. Our prayers may not be answered in the way we would like, but God still hears them. The lesson for us all is that we do not need to be alone. God is always with us and we can talk to Him and ask for His love and guidance. This is what we have taught our children.

Both Richard and I attended Catholic elementary and secondary schools. Our religious beliefs had been ingrained and reaffirmed in us by our educational and church systems. As a young boy, Richard had even been an altar server. If we both truly believed what we had been taught—that God is the God of the impossible, that miracles do happen, and He can cure the sick—then at this time we had to embrace the power of prayer.

I truly believe that it does not matter what your religious belief system may be. It does not matter if you are part of an organized religion or not. There is a spiritual reality that transcends the physical. When we believe in something greater than ourselves, a power or an energy, it can be tapped into for strength, comfort, and support. It is a power that can soothe the soul, lift the spirits, and grace us with peace of mind. It is the same energy that nurtures the entire earth. Prayer can open the door to allow this healing power in. For us, that power was God.

We were dealing with the medical reality that our son was going to die. When we said that we had to pray, we meant it. We had never seen a miracle or, if we had, we had never identified it as such. Yet, we believed in the possibility of miracles. We believed God could do all things. Our hope was that God would answer our prayers and heal our son. Every possible scientific and medical effort was being done; but, given the prognosis of the pathology of this type of cancer, this would not be enough.

Because of the severity of the prognosis, the doctors had to work quickly. Hours after being admitted, Steven was prepped and taken to the operating room to undergo the biopsies and preliminary tests. A section of the tumour on Steven's neck was removed in order to microscopically confirm the diagnosis. During this examination, cells were seen and identified as cancerous. This observation fit the criteria of the clinical suspicion of neuroblastoma.

Previous to making a decision regarding treatment, the disease had to be staged. Steven's oncologist had to determine how far along the cancer had advanced in order to know what could be done as far as treatment. Steven had to undergo a bone marrow biopsy and an aspiration of his hip, and he had to endure the insertion of a Hickman catheter. The biopsy and aspiration would be indicative of the stage Steven's cancer was in. The catheter was inserted in anticipation of chemotherapy. Neuroblastoma in children advances at a rapid rate. If anything could be done for Steven, it would have to be done expediently.

Tuesday evening, just twenty-four hours after seeing our family doctor, Steven was in the operating room having the procedures completed. Although we did not ask anyone to come, twenty-two members of our families had gathered and were waiting in the Intensive Care Unit lounge with us. Although Steven was not in the Intensive Care Unit, our large family was offered this lounge so we could all be together.

Several family members went to our home to be with Laura and Ryan. So many of our loved ones dropped whatever they were doing to help us. Our home was filled with love and prayers. My mother and my sister immediately moved into our home to keep it running. Laura, who was five, and Ryan who was only two, were unaware of the seriousness of the circumstances, but they felt the fear around them. Since Richard and I were spending so much time away from home, they knew something was wrong.

While Steven was recovering from the anesthetic, the pediatric oncologist came into the lounge and addressed the members of our family. Speaking to Richard and me he asked, "Shall I speak to you both privately, or shall I tell everyone here our findings?"

Tell all of us together," Richard and I responded. We knew the seriousness of what he was going to tell us. The love and support of our families was extremely important to us and would help get us through all of this, no matter what the outcome.

"I'm sorry to have to say this," he began, "but Steven has the form of cancer known as neuroblastoma. We will have to confirm the diagnosis in the morning, of course, but at this point in time, he has the bad one." All of the family heard what this expert said. In a very serious tone, he told us, "He will be dead in three to twelve months."

At this point, the medical profession and experts in pediatric oncology were offering us no hope for Steven's survival. Nevertheless, we had to entertain the possibility of some form of hope. We realized and believed that we must not give up hope.

One of Richard's brothers, a non-physician, asked, "What do we do now?"

"We pray," Richard responded.

His brother persisted, "No, but what do we do? What do we do for Steven?"

Again, Richard replied, "We pray." Richard continued, "We pray, because if he has what they say then he is going to die. We can do all the things we have to do medically, but it's not going to be enough to save Steven. These medical experts are the best in their fields and they aren't giving us any hope."

The atmosphere in the waiting room was bleak. Everyone was either weeping or white with shock. Richard simply said, "Let's start a prayer."

At that very moment, as if choreographed by powers above, Father Con, our parish priest, walked into the room. Richard gave him a synopsis of the situation and explained the prognosis based on the biopsy results. I added that we were just beginning a prayer and asked Father Con if he would lead us.

We initially did not recognize the amazing "coincidence" of Father Con arriving at the exact moment we were to pray. Just like the night we got the phone call from our family doctor, Father Con's timing was uncanny. It was as if God was orchestrating things and making Himself present. It was as if He was walking with us at the times we needed Him the most.

Father Con told us that he thought this was a remarkable experience—a family with two brothers who are doctors, sitting in the hospital, having just been told devastating news. Instead of saying, "Let's get another medical opinion," they said, "Let's get a God-opinion; let's get God to help us here." And that is what we did. We prayed.

◊ ◊ ◊

Before the ordeal of discovering Steven's lump, other than a prayer before a meal, our family was not in the habit of praying aloud together. Richard and I had never actually come together as a couple to pray. We had always been private with our prayers. Richard and I, like many other people, had done things by rote. We went to church regularly. We celebrated Christmas and Easter. We did all the things that were supposed to be done within our faith. But, that night, in Steven's hospital room, alone together after all of our family members had left and as Steven slept in his bed, Richard and I prayed like we had never prayed before.

We had a terminally ill child, who was flesh of our flesh. We had to do whatever we could to keep him alive. We were baring our very souls to each other and to God. Our love for our child bound us together on a heightened spiritual level as we put our son's life in His hands. We prayed for the strength to accept whatever God's will was to be. We wanted Steven to be saved. We wanted him healed. Who wouldn't, as a parent? But, we also knew that if Steven was not to live, then we needed God to stay with us, be with us, guide us, and show us what this was all about. Our prayer was that we would not blame God for what was happening. We would not forsake God. We knew we needed Him and that He would have to be with us constantly. It was a really heart-felt prayer. This was a conversation with God that came from our hearts.

The prayer we said that night was this:

Thank You for the gift of our son and for the seven years
we have been privileged to have had him.
Dear God, please heal our son. Save his life.
If he is not to live, please Lord, stay with us and hold our hands.
Be with us and guide us, and show us what this is all about.
We will not blame or forsake You.
We need You and we ask for You to be with us constantly.
We will find some good in this. And that is a hard thing to do.
But it is the right thing to do.
Above all, Thy will be done. Amen

We decided to take turns staying with Steven in his hospital
room. That night, Richard stayed beside Steven on a cot that the
nurse brought in, while I went home to Laura and Ryan.

It was important for Richard that we make Steven's stay in the
hospital as non-traumatic as possible. The next day, as requested,
I brought in a red sweater for Richard and wore one myself.
Richard and I wore the same red sweaters everyday for the duration of Steven's stay, and every night we washed them at home so
they would be ready for the next day. It was so Steven would not
realize how long he had been in the hospital. We are not sure if it
worked, but it was for him. We wanted to do everything we could
to make sure that Steven was alright, physically and emotionally.

◊ ◊ ◊

From that day forward, we got really serious about getting help
from God. We asked many people to pray. We decided that we
had to have a structure so we enlisted everybody we knew to pray
for Steven. We called our relatives; our extended family; our
friends; Steven's school; our church; two convents, The Sisters of
St. Joseph and The Sisters of the Precious Blood Monastery; colleagues at the college where I taught; many of Richard's patients;
and Richard's staff. There was an incredible ripple effect. Each

person contacted by us contacted someone else, and so on, and so on. Many interdenominational prayer chains grew out of our very public requests for Steven's returned health.

We have many stories of those who put immense effort into their prayers for our family. In particular was Sister St. Brigid, of the Sisters of St. Joseph, a delightful ninety-three-year-old patient of Richard's. Many people believed that she had a "direct line to God" and, therefore, was specifically asked to pray for Steven. She asked for a picture of Steven in order to visualize his healing as part of her meditation. She was an unbelievable woman. She prayed for twenty-four hours straight, to the point where the Superior General of the convent called Richard and asked if Sister St. Brigid could go to bed. Richard responded, "I think you can leave her be." He knew Sister St. Brigid was elderly but that she was strong in faith; and she, herself, would recognize the time to rest.

In Richard's medical practice, many patients prayed for Steven. To this day, we are so grateful for everyone's prayers. One of the poignant stories that still stands out in our minds is that of one patient, a man who was a truck driver. He had not been down on his knees to pray in years. He came in to Richard's office one day and said, "I heard about your son, Dr. Rick, and I got down on my knees last night and I prayed for him." The one thing this man could do, in Richard's time of need, was pray. And although it was not easy for this patient, for whatever reason, he had done it. Richard had helped this patient and his family over the years, and he was touched by the selfless prayer. After years of taking care of his patients, many patients were giving back by praying for us.

The ripple effect continued. There were so many prayers that you could literally feel the strength of them. It was the power of these prayers that uplifted us and gave us the strength to keep going. Richard and I were not eating much. We were not sleeping. We were simply moving through time. I am the type of person who cannot function without regular sleep, and yet I was able to keep going. I know, with certainty, that the prayers sustained us. We could sense it. We could feel it. It was like being carried through this unbearable experience by something unseen–something beyond us.

During this time, my friend Barbara gave me the poem "Footprints" by Margaret Fishback Powers. This poem exemplifies much of what we felt was happening.

FOOTPRINTS

One night a man had a dream. He dreamed he was walking along the beach with the LORD. Across the sky flashed scenes from his life. For each scene, he noticed two sets of footprints in the sand: One belonged to him, and the other to the LORD.

When the last scene of his life flashed before him, he looked back at the footprints in the sand. He noticed that many times along the path of his life there was only one set of footprints. He also noticed that it happened at the very lowest and saddest times in his life.

This really bothered him and he questioned the LORD about it.

"LORD, you said that once I decided to follow you, you'd walk with me all the way. But I have noticed that during the most troublesome times in my life, there is only one set of footprints. I don't understand why when I needed you most you would leave me."

The LORD replied, "My precious, precious child, I love you and I would never leave you. During your times of trial and suffering, when you see only one set of footprints, it was then that I carried you."

Footprints, originally titled, "I Had A Dream," was written by Margaret Fishback Powers at Echo Lake Bible Camp, near Kingston, Ontario during a Colour Weekend Youth Retreat in 1964.

CHAPTER THREE

edical Procedures - Trust

Richard was an intern in pediatrics when Steven was born. During the months leading up to Steven's birth, he saw a lot of things happen. He delivered babies and had seen those who were stillborn and babies who had died shortly after birth. He was also involved with dying children. He assisted parents and helped them cope with their personal trauma after the loss of a child. His medical studies exposed him to life and death.

When Steven was born, Richard cried tears of joy and gratitude that our son was healthy. When Richard left the labour room to tell my mother of our new arrival, she thought his tears were those of only joy. Richard explained that they were more than that. He was overwhelmed by a sadness that was hard to understand, and that surprised even him. He knew that where there was life, there would eventually be death. We just do not know when.

Richard's love for Steven was intense from the very beginning. He was totally enthralled with his first-born. Richard had a very special bond with him. It was an unusually close relationship, even for a father and son. Richard spent every moment of his free time teaching Steven songs, reciting the alphabet, and all those special things that come with parenthood. Over the years, this strong bond included a trusting love between the two of them. It was completely a situation of "I trust you, and you trust me." Richard always challenged Steven but never to the point that he would be put in harm's way.

There we were, going through this serious medical experience with Steven, and it was the relationship of unquestioning trust between him and his father that helped get Steven through it. I was not allowed in the rooms for the medical procedures, but Richard, as a doctor, was permitted to accompany Steven throughout the course of every procedure and to the start of any surgery. There were some very painful procedures that Steven had to endure. Throughout all of it, he trusted everything that his father said to him and everything he asked him to do.

On Wednesday, Steven had to have a lumbar puncture and a myelogram to determine the spread of the cancer. During a lumbar puncture, spinal fluid is taken from the spine for analysis of cancer cells. During a myelogram, dye is administered to outline the spinal cord to look further for any invasion of cancer. These are both very painful and frightening tests. They had to be done previous to any surgery to remove the tumour in Steven's chest. To lessen Steven's discomfort, only Richard lifted him to and from his bed, the gurneys, and the X-ray tables. The practice of having only one person handle him allowed Steven to be lifted in an anticipated way. This process reduced Steven's interaction with well-intentioned, but unfamiliar, hospital staff. There was no jerking or unnecessary pain. He trusted his dad and was so brave through it all.

◊ ◊ ◊

The procedure room itself was frightening enough for a seven-year-old boy. There was a narrow table with a marble-like top. A white cloth that was spread over it barely separated Steven from the coldness of the tabletop. Above the table hung a large metal piece of grey machinery. It moved laterally, back and forth, in close range of Steven's small body as it took the X-rays. The rays of the machine passed through our son and into the film below the table.

The table sat in the middle of a large but cramped room. There were hospital carts and trays of medical tools everywhere. Through a big glass window was an ominous-looking wall of dials and gauges. The X-ray technicians stood behind the window, protected against the dangers of radiation. There they could monitor the patient and observe the procedure while safely operating the instruments. Four technicians, a radiologist, a radiologist resident, and a nurse were behind the glass wall. In spite of the exposure to the radiation, Richard, wearing a lead apron to offer him some protection, stood right beside Steven, and held his hand as the X-rays were being taken. Richard wondered if Steven realized he had no apron and no glass to shield him.

Our poor little boy was going through so much. He had a wound on his neck from the biopsy, a puncture in his chest for the catheter, and a sore hip from the bone biopsy. Now he had to go through the lumbar puncture and myelogram.

"Well, we are going to hold him down for this test. You can explain to him what we're going to do," a technician announced to Richard.

"Why are you going to hold him down?" Richard asked.

"Because it hurts a lot," the technician answered.

"Yeah, I know, but why are you going to hold him down?" Richard questioned.

"He'll move," the technician replied.

"I know it is going to hurt, but he doesn't have to move," Richard continued.

"He's only a little boy. They usually move," the technician said.

"I'll just tell him not to move," Richard concluded.

Richard explained the procedure for the myelogram to Steven. "A needle will be inserted into your back and it will hurt. You might want to yell, scream, kick, and jump, but if you do any of these things, they'll have to hold you down. If you decide that you can lie here and not move, the test can be done much more simple and without you having to be restrained."

During a lumbar puncture, the patient must lie extremely still. Normally, the staff must restrain children so they do not move. Moving could have dire consequences. Steven did not want to be strapped or held down; neither did his father. Richard explained to Steven the seriousness of moving his tiny body during this possibly painful procedure. Because a needle had to be inserted and "threaded" between two adjoining lumbar vertebrae, movement could easily damage tissue and nerves. Strengthened by his complete trust in his father, Steven assured him that he would remain motionless during the procedure as long as he could hold his dad's hand.

Richard's mantra is that we always have a choice in the way we respond to a situation–we only have control of own behaviour. Steven chose to respond to his pain by lying still, on his own, and unrestrained.

Steven, an admirable little trooper, said he could take the pain. Richard told Steven that while they held each other's hand Steven's pain would leave him and go into his dad's hand. In this way, Richard would share the pain and absorb it into his own body. "We've been through a lot and we can get through this," Richard said to Steven.

Steven asked, "But Daddy, what if this pain is more than both of us can handle?"

Richard responded, "It'll go right through my feet, into the ground, and all the way to China. China is so far away that we'll be OK."

Steven looked up at his father and saw the six-foot-two-inch, strong and powerful man ready to protect him. "Alright," Steven said to his dad.

Richard turned to the technicians, "All right, we'll do it. Don't hold him. He's going to be alright on his own."

"Are you sure he's not going to move?" they asked.

"I'm not going to move," Steven said to all those in the room.

As the technicians got ready to begin the procedure, Steven held up a hand. "Dad, just give me a second." Richard knew that Steven wanted time to say a prayer. "OK, I'm ready," Steven said after opening his eyes.

As they started the myelogram, some of the technicians had tears well up in their eyes. To their disbelief, Steven did not move. There was no need to restrain him and the procedure went smoothly.

Symbolically for Steven, the pain was leaving his body and going far away. When Richard told me about this, we could picture the pain being drawn out of Steven and being displaced beyond him. Looking back I see the further symbolism of Richard's actions. Here, a father told his son that when they held each other's hand, the pain would be taken away.

In the scriptures, God carries and protects us.

I will not forget you. I have held you in the palm of my hand.

Isaiah 49:15-16

◊ ◊ ◊

There we were with our seven-year-old son, who was diagnosed with a terrible disease. We had been told that he was going to die, yet there were many tests and procedures to be endured to confirm that diagnosis. The grapefruit-sized tumour in his chest had to be dealt with by surgical removal, or de-bulking, and, possibly, radiation therapy. Steven had already been prepared for chemotherapy with the Hickman catheter. At best, these treatments would extend his life by only a few weeks or months.

On Wednesday, Steven went through all kinds of tests. One such test was the 2-D echocardiogram, which is an ultrasound of the heart to assess the function of the heart valves and muscle. The chest tumour was right behind Steven's heart. If they were to give radiation to that area, they would have to radiate through the heart. The heart would be damaged; therefore, they had to make sure the heart was functioning properly before they could begin treatment. This test would also be used as a base line to compare how his heart was functioning once radiation had begun. The echocardiogram would enable the doctors to monitor any changes that occurred as a result of radiotherapy.

Other tests Steven had to endure included blood tests, a CAT scan and X-rays of his abdomen, and X-rays of his head. An intra-venous pyelogram (IVP) was also administered. In this procedure a dye is injected into the veins leading to the kidneys, bladder, and related organs of the urinary tract to determine if there are any other tumours or obstructions.

Somehow, they missed testing his adrenal glands. As his tumour could have originated from the adrenal glands, the doctors needed to perform a second CAT scan of Steven's abdomen. Richard and Steven were sent by ambulance to another hospital for the second CAT scan, as the machine used earlier that day on Steven had to be repaired. In order to monitor Steven's Hickman catheter, the hospital assigned a nurse to accompany them. When they returned to the hospital, the nurse mysteriously disappeared.

Upon their return, we were told that the doctors wanted to do another test on Steven's kidneys. We were especially concerned because the test required another dose of dye. Steven's body had endured a lot of dye from the tests administered only hours earlier.

Although further testing had to be done, we were told that more dye could cause further complications for Steven. However, in the interest of time, and because of the urgency of the situation, the test needed to be done immediately to see if the cancer had spread to the kidneys. Weighing the risks, Richard signed the appropriate forms.

Richard and Steven were sent into the same procedure room they were in the day before. The technicians were ready for him and soon began administering the dye. In order to monitor the dye travelling through his kidneys the technicians took an X-ray that was followed a few minutes later by another one. I was extremely worried and deeply concerned about the number of X-rays Steven had been exposed to over the previous forty-eight hours.

While Richard was beside Steven throughout the procedure, my mother and I were sitting outside the procedure room, keeping a faithful vigil. Steven's neck was bandaged from the biopsy done on his neck; the Hickman catheter was in his chest, ready to receive the chemotherapy if need be; his hip was sore from the bone marrow test; and his back was taped from the lumbar puncture. Yet, Steven was quietly going through this X-rays, likely sleeping from exhaustion.

While Richard was walking the perimeter of the room in an attempt to maintain a sense of presence for his son as well as to ward off sleep, he started staring at the walls. To this day, Richard recalls them being pale green in colour. A sense of calm enveloped him. Needing to share this emotion, he came out to the hall where my mother and I were praying.

"He's going to be fine," Richard told us.

I asked the obvious, "How do you know?"

He replied, "I haven't got a clue. I just know he is going to be fine."

Richard was not sure that he understood what was happening, but he was sure that God had somehow touched him with the understanding that his son would be fine. This was a very powerful feeling for Richard. It moved him from a state of despair to the sense of hope that Steven would live.

"I think I understand. God, in someway, touched me," Richard said and then returned to take care of our son.

Unbeknownst to us, Father Don Sanvido, a friend of Richard's, was standing in a waiting room beside the procedure room. He had been standing very patiently, praying for the duration of Steven's procedure. When it was done, Richard came out and was told by a nurse that a friend was in the waiting room and would like to see him. When Richard saw Father Sanvido, he thanked him for his visit and prayers. After Father Sanvido left, Richard reiterated to us the "coincidence" of Father Sanvido's timing, in light of Richard's overwhelming recent feeling that Steven would be alright and would live. We did not overlook the sign: Father Don's surname means "with life." Once again, God was with us and was giving us the signs and the hope we needed.

To our amazement, the test results showed that everything was clear. In our prayers, we had asked that every test would be fine. Astoundingly, every test came back with normal results. Other than the original test that showed cancerous cells in the neck tumour, no other test showed any sign that the cancer had spread. The tests did not detect tumours anywhere else in Steven's body. For me, these results created a wonderful hope, a hope that had not been offered by the medical team.

◊ ◊ ◊

That night, the attending doctor came to us and said that the nurse who accompanied Richard and Steven in the ambulance had developed a rash. She was sent to see the dermatologist in the hospital. We were told that it was very likely to be chicken pox.

This news was not good. Steven was being prepped for chemotherapy; chemotherapy suppressed the immune system. If Steven had to start chemotherapy in the very near future, it would make it harder for Steven to fight the chicken pox if he had been exposed to it. With a weakened immune system, the chicken pox virus would go rampant throughout Steven's body. Our fear was that Steven could die sooner. The doctor administered Immune Globulin Serum to kill the virus, if it was in his system. As Steven was being given the serum, Richard and I prayed in his hospital room.

It was about 10:30 p.m. and only Steven, Richard, and I were in Steven's hospital room. Relatives who had visited that evening had left the hospital. Richard and I began to pray from the depths of our hearts.

Our desire is that, if it is Thy will, Lord, please heal our son, Steven.
If Steven is to be taken from us, then help us, so that we will not forsake You.
We pray that You walk with us throughout this difficult time.
We thank You for the gift of Steven.
We have enjoyed seven wonderful years and fervently pray to enjoy many more years with him.

As we concluded our prayer, Steven began shaking and sweating. He burned with fever. Richard told me that Steven was having a reaction to the Immune Globulin Serum that had just been administered. His temperature went from normal to very high in a matter of a minute. Richard buzzed the intercom and called in the nurse to take Steven's temperature. Finding it extremely high, the nurse turned to Richard, "What would you have me do?" she asked Richard as if he were the attending doctor.

Richard responded, "Just follow your normal protocol." She administered a fever-reducing medication, took his temperature a second time, asked if we would like something to drink or eat, and left the room. We all knew it would take approximately fifteen to thirty minutes for the medication to take effect. Because Steven was shaking so badly, I moved to his bedside to wipe his forehead. Richard and I continued to pray. I tried to calm Steven by passing my hands over his forehead and gently stroking his body. My intention was to comfort him. As I stroked Steven and prayed over him, I felt his skin suddenly go cool under my hands. Although the nurse had only administered the medication minutes earlier, he stopped shaking and his temperature returned to normal. I did not understand what had happened, just that it had happened. When the nurse came in, we told her about the rapid change in Steven's temperature. Her response was, "Boy, I've never seen that medication work so quickly." Richard and I looked at each other and agreed, "Neither have we." We were amazed. We did not identify the significance of what had transpired in those moments until days later.

In retrospect, there was such peace and calm in Steven's room at that time. I know God was there. He was using us to calm Steven down. I feel that I was an instrument for His healing. Because I was open and believed, God was there to help us. At the time, I thought that this was another sign that Steven was going to be alright. God's presence was in the room that night. The feeling we had was that God was with us and we could get through it. We would get through it.

◊ ◊ ◊

Steven had not yet had his operation to remove the chest tumour. We were unaware of what was still ahead of us. When I was continuing to be the optimist, Richard, the realist, had to resist thoughts of Steven lying in a coffin. His medical training told him that this child was going to die. Richard was trying to

Our Story

hold on to his hope, but he had never seen anything like this happen before.

Every time the pediatric oncologist entered Steven's room, he seemed extremely negative. He carried a medical textbook about cancer in children, and laid it on Steven's bed. We had never told Steven that he had cancer or that he might die. This doctor was potentially exposing our son to a negative outcome that we had not yet accepted. The doctor's insensitive approach irritated me immensely. If Steven wanted to, he could have read the title of the book. The oncologist's message was clear: "The child has got cancer. Just stop denying it. You know the child's got it. You're going to have to accept it sooner or later." It got to the point where I told Richard that I wanted that man out of Steven's room. "I don't like what he brings into this room, Rick. It's a negative force. I can't handle it. He has absolutely no hope that Steven will survive this disease. I need some hope."

Neither the oncologist nor Richard had ever known of a child to survive a diagnosis such as this. Yet, Richard and I believed that God could do anything. We continued to pray. Throughout our ordeal, Richard and I took turns staying in Steven's hospital room.

Because I still wanted to make sure things were alright with Laura and Ryan, I went home again that night and Richard stayed with Steven.

After going to bed, I found myself going to the Bible for comfort. I simply opened it up to a random page. Since Steven had been admitted, for some reason, time after time, the Bible kept opening to John 16:23-24. According to *The Living Bible,* "At that time you won't need to ask me for anything, for you can go directly to the Father and ask Him, and he will give you what you ask for because you use my name. Ask, using my name, and you will receive, and your cup of joy will overflow." In this passage, Jesus is instructing His disciples. It was my understanding that I could petition to God the Father, in the name of Jesus, to claim healing for Steven. It would then be in God's hands. The passage, "Ask and you shall receive" is a matter of petitioning. We must have the courage to ask and know that we are worthy to ask. We must then also be prepared to accept God's will.

The image of being in the palm of God's hand, from Isaiah 49:15, is powerfully strong. Anything you ask of your heavenly Father will be given to you just as you would be granted a request by your earthly father, but only if it is good for you. Therefore, God's will is important in this because God is aware of the impact of your request upon your whole life and the effects, one way or the other, of the request. In some way, these events impact heavily on the rest of our lives. Some requests do not have the desired happy ending. However, there is always growth.

I would not wish our experience with Steven on anyone. Yet, I would not want to have missed it because a lot of learning happened in a very short time. Our faith, our belief in God, and our trust in Him was shown to us. His love was brought home to us. He was indeed there in our hour of need.

I also remember praying to God that whatever the lesson He wanted us to learn, we would learn it quickly and grow so that Steven would have a chance to live.

CHAPTER FOUR

earts Full of Hope

"Hope springs eternal in the human breast. Man never is, but always to be blest." - Alexander Pope

Alexander Pope's reflection from his Essay on Man is indicative of what direction man's heart takes when the scientific or medical world does not offer a positive solution.

The *Concise Oxford Dictionary (10th ed.)* defines "hope" as "to look with expectation and desire, clinging to a mere possibility." That is exactly what we were doing–clinging to a mere possibility.

The next time I saw Richard at the hospital, I firmly told him that we had the power to claim Jesus to heal Steven. I enthused, "You know if it doesn't happen, if it's not His will, we will have to accept that. But, you know we have to ask. We have to try." I kept having an overwhelming feeling of hope. Richard, of course, had a foot in each camp. There was the medical world, the realistic and scientific world, which pointed to the statistical inevitability of a negative outcome. Yet he, too, hoped that divine intervention would prevail in granting our son's returned health.

Our constant struggle was the reality of what was supposed to happen medically, juxtaposed with the knowledge that we could go beyond the medical world for divine help. I felt that we could not go down without the best fight that we could fight on Steven's behalf. We had to use every atom of our beings. Everything we had ever internalized through readings, studies, or experience pointed to the knowledge that there was something beyond us. This "something beyond us", in the unseen reality, was what we had to tap into. We had to keep up our hope and trust in this unseen reality. We were hoping against hope that all would be well. We were clinging to a mere possibility. We had been primed for this experience. Every part of our beings worked toward a positive outcome.

◊ ◊ ◊

On the day of Steven's appointment with our pediatric oncologist, I had to quickly do a re-evaluation of my life. I had to re-prioritize my life and be with my children. I knew that I couldn't go back to work at the college at this time. I was granted a leave of absence from where I had been teaching for over a ten-year period after requesting time off to be with my family. I did not know how long I would be off, but as time went on I felt the need to be home with my children for an extended period. Although I had worked so hard to get my position, I had three babies at home who needed me. I needed to be a part of my children's lives in a way that working at the college did not afford me. The realization hit me like a ton of bricks.

A month after Steven was first diagnosed, I resigned from my teaching position at the college. Because I loved my job, the decision to leave was the result of much soul-searching. Steven and the other children needed me. Considering all the nurturing Steven would need, as well as the support Steven's siblings would require to get through their brother's illness, made my decision necessary. During the emotional upheaval of Steven's illness, Richard left his practice for two weeks starting the day we went to the specialist's office. The idea was to focus on the process of getting our child well.

It was the prayers that helped us through. We were grateful for the continued prayers and support of friends, relatives, colleagues, patients, schools, and parishes. We even encouraged them to use Steven's name when praying because we had been told that directed prayer was important.

◊ ◊ ◊

The results of the myelogram were inconclusive. If the tumour had been sharing a blood supply with the spine, removing the tumour could compromise the blood supply to the spinal cord. Lack of blood could cause the spinal cord to swell. In that case, not only would we have a child with a terrible cancer, and one who would possibly have to undergo chemotherapy, he could be paralysed from that level of the spine down. If the tumour and the spinal cord had a common blood supply, the doctors would have to operate on Steven's spine first to remove some of the bone around the spinal cord. That way, if the cord swelled it would not compress against the bone and he would not be paralysed.

Because the tests were inconclusive, the doctors did not know if there was a shared blood supply and, therefore, had to do more CAT scans on Steven's back. After these scans, it was finally determined that the tumour and the spine did not share a common blood supply. The doctors would not have to operate on his spine prior to removing the chest tumour. One less operation, one less complication: another prayer answered.

Looking back, I realize the significance of the spiritual things that were happening. On the first day in hospital, we were given a pathology report that confirmed that Steven had neuroblastoma. We were told that our child was in trouble. We had prayed for discrepancy. We knew that concrete decisions could not be made in the imperfect science of medicine unless there was certainty and confidence shown by test results. Doctors need hard facts to make decisions. They do not like discrepancy. We knew that with discrepancy, things would not be quite so clear and that the diagnosis could then morph to a less malignant disease; perhaps, even further, to a benign disease. We did not believe that the physicians involved would be able to accept the change from a malignant to a benign disease in one big jump. They would need time to digest any changes that were occurring.

◊ ◊ ◊

With such a devastating diagnosis, our only hope was to focus on some doubt in the type of cancer Steven had. We accepted that he had cancer and that it was serious, but we were not prepared to lose our son without a fight. Prayers were our weapons. Once we started praying and got the prayer chain in action, we heard the doctors mention that Steven's illness may alternatively be a T-cell lymphoma. Even this would be a very serious cancer to have. With T-cell lymphoma, Steven had a 75 percent chance of survival after three years of chemotherapy. With a neuroblastoma, the chances of survival were virtually non-existent in a seven-year-old boy. At this point, we were getting the slightest hint of discrepancy in the diagnosis. Were our prayers starting to be answered already?

Surgery to remove the tumour from Steven's chest had been scheduled for Thursday morning. We were told that the doctors were fully expecting to find the tumour to be malignant, which would confirm their diagnosis of a neuroblastoma.

Richard met with the surgeon who had the task of removing Steven's tumour. As the surgeon explained the procedure, Richard asked what the surgeon's thoughts were on the chance of the chest tumour being unrelated to the neck tumour and if he thought there was much chance of the chest tumour being benign.

The surgeon looked Richard square in the eye and almost apologetically said, "It would be idiocy to entertain a diagnosis that these two tumours are unrelated and that either are benign." Richard told me that after a second of pause and reflection, he responded to the surgeon, a long time friend, "Then this patient has an idiot for a father." The surgeon acknowledged their disagreement and continued on with his explanation of the upcoming surgery.

However, we were still getting very little hope from the medical community for our child's ultimate survival. The doctors were telling us that there was no chance of the chest tumour being benign. They had estimated their degree of accuracy to be 99.9 percent.

◊ ◊ ◊

On Thursday morning, the surgery to take the grapefruit-sized tumour out of Steven's chest began. Needless to say, we were praying. My mother, my mother-in-law, and I held hands in prayer as Steven was being wheeled into surgery. This was a powerful triad of love. We prayed for God to guide the surgeon's hands. Our prayer was spontaneous, beautiful, and heartfelt. It was so powerful and came from a place of love, earnestness, and faith. I felt as though the words were divinely given to me. On that day, in that operating room lounge, there was a spiritual presence that directed the prayer.

We felt so fortunate that Richard was a doctor; he was able to explain the surgery and the procedures to Steven. His position allowed him to be with little Steven right into the operating room. They looked at each other, Richard supportively and Steven trustingly, until the anaesthetic was administered and Steven fell into a coma-like sleep. With a quick kiss to his son's cheek, Richard left our son in the care of the surgical team and to God and came to sit with us in the operating room lounge.

As Richard brought Steven into the operating room, many operating staff members were overcome with tears. Most of the staff were Richard's professional colleagues. They saw their associate, a doctor, as an anxious parent, escorting his son into the operating theatre. The prognosis before the surgery was that this young child was likely to die due to this illness.

Because the chest tumour was situated near the aorta and close to the spine, the surgeon had to take care not to nick the aorta, the main artery from the heart. The surgeon went into Steven's chest from the left side of his back, not from the front. Ribs had to be moved to get into the chest cavity. In such a tiny body, the surgery was both delicate and difficult.

In the operating room waiting area were the parents of a boy, about ten- or eleven- years old, who was in the adjoining operating suite to Steven. This boy was undergoing surgery to remove a brain tumour. The operation had extended four hours longer than anticipated. The parents were visibly upset and obviously lacking information on the status of their son. Richard and I empathized with these people. We wanted to say something encouraging to them, yet we were too upset and preoccupied thinking of Steven. We continued to pray for Steven and included the other little boy in surgery in our prayers. His prognosis was not favourable either.

Halfway through Steven's operation, Richard and I noticed two members of Steven's operating team rush out of the operating room. "Hey, those doctors are supposed to be in there working on Steven!" Richard exclaimed. Richard concluded that they must have had an emergency on the ward that they had been told to attend.

As they ran by the lounge door they turned around, popped their heads in, and said, "Dr. Zizzo, do you want to come here for a second?" As Richard approached them, they showed him a K-basin with a towel over it.

"We have Steven's tumour in our hands," they said.

"Why?" Richard asked.

"We're going to do a frozen section," they replied.

"No frozen sections! There is a lot of controversy around what is in his neck. I had been told that there would be no frozen sections," Richard said. He felt strongly about this decision because a frozen section is only a partial analysis of the entire tumour. Richard would have rather had the whole tumour analysed before any decisions were made regarding further treatments for Steven.

"Take a look at it," the younger doctor suggested. The doctors removed the towel from the K-basin to allow Richard to view the tissue. He looked at it and then asked the doctors to turn it over. The tumour was very large. Like the pediatric oncologist had said, it was the size of a grapefruit.

"That looks benign!" Richard exclaimed. The tumour was fully encapsulated and had no indication of spread.

"That is what the surgeon said," remarked the doctors.

"But why then are you still going to do a frozen section?" Richard asked.

"Everyone is so excited about the possibility that this could be benign!" one of the doctors said as though it was obvious. Richard's colleagues were excited that there was a chance that Steven's initial prognosis may not be accurate. If the tumour turned out to be benign, the final diagnosis would change.

Richard returned to the issue of the frozen section. "Are you sure you want to do this? You want a frozen section?" Richard asked the doctors as they began to walk towards the pathology room where the conclusion would be made.

"Yes, they want to take a look. They want to be sure," a doctor responded over her shoulder.

A few minutes later, an older doctor came out of the operating room pathology area. Richard was still standing in the hallway, contemplating the new information. This doctor, a pediatric pathologist, had been Richard's medical advisor during his years in medical school. Richard was surprised to see him because the doctor was supposed to be on staff at a hospital in western Canada.

"What are you doing here?" Richard asked upon seeing him.

"I work here again," the doctor responded, instantly recognizing Richard.

"I didn't know you were back!" Richard said.

"That's not important, right now. I looked at your son's tumour," the pathologist said to brush away Richard's line of conversation and focus on the task at hand.

"Really? What did you find?" Richard queried.

"It's benign. I'd stake my reputation on it. I sliced it from one end to the other and there is not a cancer cell in there," the doctor said victoriously.

"Thank God," was all Richard could say.

"You're not out of the woods, yet. I took another look at the initial neck biopsy slide. The first chance I had to look at it was today. It's a T-cell lymphoma. He still has cancer," the pathologist continued.

Although the doctor was not aware of it, his words added one more page to our "Book of Hope." The diagnosis was moving away from the death sentence we were given only days earlier.

Steven's doctors told us that this was a neuroblastoma at the beginning of the week, and they told us that there was no chance that this tumour could be benign, let alone be different from the one in his neck. Now everything that we had prayed for had come to pass. We knew that Steven was not out of the woods yet, but we were filled with hope. Our prayers for discrepancy were being answered.

"Rick," the pediatric pathologist said, "Steven still has cancer, and we are going to have to deal with it the best way we can."

Richard wanted to be a witness to the conversation between the doctors who were deciding Steven's course of treatment. "I want to be there when you inform the surgeon. You don't mind, do you?" Richard asked his friend and former advisor.

"No, not at all. Come with me," was the pathologist's reply. Richard wanted to make sure that he was hearing the diagnosis firsthand.

Together, Richard and the pathologist went into the restricted area before the actual operating theatre. The pathologist pushed a button on an intercom and asked for the pediatric surgeon by name.

"Yeah, I'm here," the pediatric surgeon replied from behind a surgical mask. He was still working on Steven.

"I've examined the specimen taken from Steven Zizzo. It is a benign ganglioneuroma. I have cut it from side to side. There's no sign of cancer," the pediatric pathologist stated.

"Thank you," was the curt reply.

From the lounge, we heard cheering from the operating room. Those of us who were waiting for Richard to return had not yet been told the good news. We were all on pins and needles with anticipation. When Richard entered to explain what the cheering was about, he could barely contain himself. "Benign!" he gasped as he walked through the door with his arms wide open.

"Thank you, Lord," was my immediate response, as I wrapped my arms around him. This was the first bit of good news that we had received during this very stressful week.

Once Richard, myself, and Steven's grandparents calmed down, Richard approached the parents of the other boy in surgery. Now that our most crucial moment was over, Richard was now able to give of himself to another set of parents who were going through the same thing. "What's happening with your son?" he asked. "I'm a doctor. You can tell me a bit about what your son is going through, if you'd like. Maybe I can shed some light on your situation. You know, just to talk for a few minutes."

Something had caused their son to have seizures and it had taken the doctors a long time to find out that it was a brain tumour. Their son was in the process of having his brain tumour surgically removed, but the doctors had not come out to tell them if it was cancerous or benign. Because the tumour had serious repercussions for the boy, malignant or benign, it had to be removed immediately.

Richard's hope was spreading to the other family. "You know it could be benign," he said. "It could be that the surgeons are taking an extra four hours because of the blood supply. The head of a child is small. Any bleeding has to be carefully suctioned and the vessels must be cauterized. These are messy procedures and the surgeons have to be very, very, very delicate in what they are doing. They do not want to hurt your son, so that could be the reason for the time extension."

An hour later the brain surgeon came out and approached the parents. "Your son's brain tumour is benign, but we had trouble with the blood vessels." And that was it! God was helping us all through. It was just amazing! Wonderful occurrences were happening that day.

In Steven's case, there was some thought that if the tumour was a form of T-cell lymphoma, there might be a chance of survival with chemotherapy treatment. This information took us from doom and gloom–with no chance of survival–to something more hopeful. God was answering our prayers. Everything we asked for–a discrepancy in the diagnosis, a benign chest tumour, and a chance at survival–had come to pass. God was indeed answering our prayers.

There had been no spread of the tumours outside of the chest and neck areas. All further tests that had been done to determine cancer spread had come back as being normal. The results were in Steven's favour. We were surviving. People were coming to our aid.

God was with us.

◊ ◊ ◊

When Steven was finally wheeled out of the operating room, lying on his left side, he had a large white dressing over the incision on the left side of his back, and there was a large tube protruding from the back of his chest to drain the fluid from the area around his lungs. In spite of his heart-wrenching appearance, we were still filled with hope.

If there is one thing that we learned throughout this ordeal, it is that a person always needs hope. No one has the right to take away another human being's hope. One can only move on by holding the hand of hope, otherwise there is despair. Hope will challenge you to believe, even at those moments when you feel that all you have left is God. In the end, you will discover that all you need is God. God is all you will ever need. There are many scriptures and psalms around the topic of hope. It is central to a human being's existence.

Remember your promise to me, your servant; it has given me hope. Even in my suffering I was comforted because your promise gave me life.

Psalm 119:49-50

There is always hope.
There is always a chance that things
are not as they appear.

CHAPTER FIVE

*E*vil Forces Versus Faith

There were many events of which we were aware. There were also some unexplained happenings, too. When we tell people about these things, they tend to look at us like we have three heads; but, there were happenings that we had trouble explaining or identifying at the time. Looking back, I think that good, as well as evil forces, were manifesting themselves. On a night that Richard stayed with Steven, something inexplicable happened.

Steven was recovering from his surgery and was confined to his bed because of all the drainage tubes. He needed attentive care. We had to help him do everything, from eating to using a bedpan. In the 1980s, hospital beds sat on castors. The bed was large and high. It had to be lifted entirely to remove it from its wheels. This action would be physically impossible for one man to do.

I had already left to go back home to be with Laura and Ryan. As Richard lowered Steven's bed, using the cranks at the foot of the bed, the bed started to fall apart. Richard got to the side of the bed just in time to catch Steven and all of his attached tubes before he fell to the floor. Just then, a nurse came running in and witnessed the bed tilting to one side as two of its wheels collapsed beneath its weight. The first wheel came off for reasons unknown. It certainly was a strange phenomenon. The bed fell to the corner with the lost wheel, causing the opposite corner to flip up and release its wheel. The nurse glared at Richard. "How did you do that?" she commanded.

Richard, still holding Steven and the tubes, was stunned. "How did I do what?" he said.

"How did you knock the wheels off the bed?" She questioned Richard as though he had done it on purpose.

"How *could* I knock the wheels off the bed?" Richard said, beginning to feel the awkwardness of Steven's body and all the medical instruments attached to it.

She questioned him further. "Well, *someone* had to do it."

Managing to maintain his juggling act, Richard retorted, "Well, I didn't do it. Get me a wheelchair!"

The nurse persisted, "What did you do?"

"Would you get me a wheelchair, please?" Richard asked, not wanting anything to fall off Steven's body while the nurse asked him silly questions.

The nurse seemed to take her time retrieving a wheelchair from down the hall. It was the first time Steven had been up and out of bed since the operation. Richard lowered Steven into the wheelchair and assured him that everything was OK. All the tubes were still in place and nothing had been disturbed. The nurse and Richard examined the bed.

"This can't happen! What happened cannot happen!" Richard said.

The nurse continued her interrogation. "What did you do?"

"Listen, honestly, I didn't do anything!" He was as bewildered as she was.

A call was made to the maintenance department to come and look at the bed. When the maintenance person came up and saw the upended bed, all he could say was, "That can't happen."

Richard looked at the nurse and said, "That's what I told you, right?" But she was not taking Richard's word for it. She did not believe the maintenance person, either.

Although the maintenance person told her that the bed could be lifted up, put back on its wheels, and would again be fine, she ordered him to remove it entirely from her ward. She did not want this incident to recur. "Get that bed out of my ward! If it happened once, it could happen again!" she assertively stated. She was not willing to admit it, but there was something weird taking place. She just did not want to say it. "I don't want this bed on my ward. Get it out of here," she insisted and made the maintenance person take it away.

If Richard had not been standing right there, Steven would have fallen to the floor and been hurt. However, because Richard was there, he was able to catch Steven and all of the wires and tubes and save him from injury. We wondered what evil forces were at work. We were convinced that there was a battle going on. We again talked to Steven about the battle. We explained that he had to be a soldier and fight. He proved to be very good at it. We also knew we had to fight it as a family. There we were, in Steven's room making extensive battle plans. We pulled paper towels from the dispenser in Steven's room, and made notes on how we were going to deal with each particular battle as it came up. This was our most earnest collaboration—we were prepared to battle until the end and not let this little guy go down without a terrific fight. We tried to anticipate and prepare for all the things that were going to happen. It was a mammoth project. We knew it was a "do or die" situation.

We used every atom of our beings to help save our child. Everything we had ever read, had ever learned, had ever believed, and everything we were—everything that was the essence of who and what Richard and Karen Zizzo were—went into saving our child. We explored all information available; Richard was able to have access to the resources available in the hospital and off-site to find out the information we needed regarding Steven's type of cancer.

We felt great comfort in knowing and believing that God was walking with us. I felt his guidance and closeness.

◊ ◊ ◊

One night after the surgery, when it was my turn to stay with Steven, he woke up screaming. What happened next was a unique and frightening experience: Steven was pushing something off him.

"Mommy, tell them to get off me! I don't want them on me! Get them off me!" he anguished, with tears in his eyes.

Something negative and evil was happening in the room. Right away I got up and began to pray furiously. I prayed with deep conviction and out loud. It was a protective prayer that came from deep within me. With my hands on Steven's shoulders in a protective fashion, I began:

This is a child of God,
I will not allow any forces other than those of the Lord to be around my son.
Jesus, please surround Steven with Your love, Your light, and Your healing.
Keep away any evil forces.
God, protect my child with Your loving grace.
Amen

I prayed for the evil in the room to leave and the light of God to shine in. Steven was fighting. He was trying to push off "the enemy." I was standing there, with my eyes wide open, and I was praying as fast and as furiously as I could. God again got me through that night.

◊ ◊ ◊

During his hospitalization, my main focus was to pray for Steven. One night as I was heading home to Laura and Ryan, praying for Steven as I drove, I had a car accident. I was just coming up to our subdivision when I stopped, with my signal on and waiting to turn left. As I looked into my rear-view mirror, I caught a glimpse of a car quickly approaching me. I realized that he was not going to stop. He was definitely going to hit me. In a split second, I had to make a decision. I was not able to turn left as intended because there was oncoming traffic, nor could I move to either side. The only thing I could do was to take my foot off the brake to lessen the impact. When the car hit me, my car lurched forward. The damage to my car was very extensive, but it could have been worse.

The police were called and quickly arrived on the scene. The driver of the other vehicle was charged with drunk driving and was put into the back of one of the police cruisers that idled nearby. Although shaken, I was able to tell the emergency personnel the events of the accident. Had I not seen the accident about to happen and not taken my foot off the brake, the force of the impact would have been much greater.

Fortunately, I only sustained an injury to my back. But the result of the injury caused severe pain for weeks to come.

I believe that everything happens for a reason. I looked at the accident and wondered why it had happened. I truly felt that evil forces were trying to take my focus away from my prayers for Steven. It was as if something was testing my convictions and my faith. I refused to allow this to happen. Over the next few weeks, I kept my focus on Steven. I gave everything I had to Steven and the battle our family had to fight. Despite my pain, I kept my faith and I kept praying. I would get through the pain.

It was God who led us through the entire ordeal. He showed us how to fight to get through it all. Looking back on it, I am just amazed that we coped so well. We really leaned on God; not feeling equipped to handle such a load. He helped us stand; when necessary, he carried us. He was always there.

Evil Forces Versus Faith

Since the ordeal of Steven's illness, our lives and our priorities changed. Our faith became so much stronger and our family became unbreakable.

CHAPTER SIX

A New Diagnosis

Steven's pediatric hematological oncologist scheduled a conference for us with Steven's team of doctors, a combination of pediatric and cancer specialists. One of their members was their spokesperson. We all sat at an oblong conference table facing one other. Richard and I sat centred on one side of the table, and the spokesperson, flanked by the doctors and interns who made up Steven's team, sat on the other side. This entire experience had started on Monday, when we first saw our family doctor. This conference was taking place on Friday. A lot had happened in these five days.

There were still many unanswered questions. These pediatric cancer experts had looked at all the slides of Steven's neck and chest tumours. They told us of the tissue situation to date. According to them, the chest tissue was benign, but the tissue in the neck was cancerous. They finally concluded that it was a T-cell lymphoma.

In retrospect, I see that the medical staff believed that we were a bit off-the-wall because we continued to say that God was answering our prayers. They insisted that we face the reality of the situation. I was told that my faith was disillusioning my view of Steven's diagnosis and that I trusted too much in prayer. They could not understand why Richard and I thought God was answering our prayers. I told them that we had prayed for discrepancy in the diagnosis and that we received that which we asked for.

The doctors introduced chemotherapy as the next course of treatment. The physicians wanted to begin a three-year course of chemotherapy that day. Richard felt that we needed the time to think this through; until we were absolutely convinced as to exactly what kind of cancer Steven had, we refused to start our child on three years of chemotherapy. Even though Richard was a physician, or perhaps because he was a physician, we wanted more answers. At this point, we were feeling that there were too many unanswered questions. In fact, everything had moved along so quickly, and there had been so many changes to the original diagnosis of neuroblastoma. We could not subject our son to chemotherapy that afternoon. People may have perceived our desire to hold off on this treatment as neglect in the care of our ill child; however, we were not convinced that the doctors had the right answers at that time.

It seemed as though the events had continued to move in the direction of our prayers. The doctors had changed Steven's diagnosis from terminal neuroblastoma to T-cell lymphoma, a cancer that does not have to be terminal. Because they now knew that the chest tumour was benign, the cancer was perceived to be only in the neck tumour. From our point of view, major decisions about Steven's life could not be made in a one-hour conference with his doctors.

It was suggested to us to equate the benign chest tumour with winning the lottery. We were told that we had won half the battle. From our point of view, however, we still had a battle on our hands. There was no time to celebrate. Now, with the changed diagnosis, we feared this life-threatening decision to start chemotherapy immediately. A three-year course of chemotherapy would have to be continued through the whole process. It could not be started and then stopped in six months. Richard was afraid that the treatment would kill Steven over the course of three years.

Steven was a typical, scrawny seven-year-old. Richard knew that chemotherapy could ravage the body. Of course, we were aware that Steven would need a course of chemotherapy, but we truly felt that we needed to wait, get all of the facts and answers, and then make the right decision.

"You can't go and give my son chemo if everything is going our way," Richard responded to the recommendation. Richard and I were convinced that unusual things were happening, which science and medicine could not explain. God was answering our prayers. Everything was happening the way we prayed it would. The test results were not what the doctors had expected. Either it was a marvellous stroke of luck, or God was really answering our prayers.

"The fact is that your son still has a neck tumour. It is big and it is a cancer, and we have all of the experts looking at it. No one will say it is benign," the spokesperson said.

"Well, nevertheless, we can't go along with chemo because we are not convinced of the final diagnosis. We won the lottery once, maybe we are going to win it again. You're not starting chemotherapy today, and that's final," was Richard's response. We needed more time to watch for further developments to help us make a decision. We still felt that God was continuing to answer our prayers.

The conference had taken an emotional toll. I could not help crying. Richard was just barely holding himself together. As I wept, an intern turned to me and slid a box of tissues across the table and simply said, "Mrs. Zizzo, your faith will get you through three years of chemotherapy."

At this point, we could not take anymore. Richard stood up, looked at me, and then he looked over at the doctors on the other side of the table. "You don't get it, do you? No chemotherapy! We're going to watch and see what happens. That's the end of this meeting." He reached down, took my hand, and headed towards the door. One doctor had a look of shock on her face. These doctors could not believe that we had the audacity to turn down chemotherapy.

"Dr. Zizzo, you are going to kill your son," called out one of the doctors before we reached the door.

"I can live with that. What I can't live with *is you* killing him," Richard responded through his tears. We left the room, still questioning whether or not we were doing the right thing. But how could we not follow our hearts? We had to acknowledge what was happening to us. There were positive messages and results, and we truly felt that God was on our side and helping our son. We had to maintain our faith. We had placed our son in the palm of God's hand and we had to trust in Him to guide us.

◊ ◊ ◊

Richard's brother, Angelo, as a family doctor, encouraged other pathologists to look at Steven's slides. Everyone agreed that the tumour in the chest was now benign. However, they could not come to a consensus about the tumour in Steven's neck. Some said that *maybe* the neck tumour was a reactive lymph node that was acting unusual. But nobody had the courage to say it was definitely benign. They told us that they were going to send the tests to other major hospitals for further verification.

One of the heads of a cancer clinic wrote back saying that he advised proceeding with the chemotherapy because he could not stake his reputation on Steven not having a malignant disease. He advised to err on the side of treating him with chemotherapy because he was not comfortable calling the tissue sample benign. He said that it just was not clear. Medicine is not a perfect science. Sometimes, you have to make a decision based on your informed, but not necessarily correct, opinion.

We felt that we needed to wait a week, or even two, to calm

down and see what was going to happen next. Would Steven get better or worse? Events had happened very quickly. The doctors wanted to treat Steven sooner, rather than later. We did not agree.

Angelo asked a specialist at his affiliate hospital for another opinion. "Who is the best person in the pathology department to look at these slides?" he asked a colleague. He was told of a female pathologist, who was a junior colleague in the pathology department and was considered very knowledgeable. That same Friday night, Angelo, called us at the hospital and informed us of the news he received from the pathologist. "I just got a call from the pathologist at the hospital," Angelo told Richard. "She said to me, 'I am sorry to have to say this…' and then she stopped, paused, and took a breath." Angelo told us that he thought that he was going to hear the worst, but she continued to say, "but I have to disagree with all of my superiors and everyone else who looked at these slides. I think that this is a benign tumour; tricky stuff, but benign."

She "could see how the other specialists would think it was a malignant disease because of the inconsistencies in so-called normal cells."

"What she saw in the slides was abnormal but still could fall into the realm of a non-malignant tumour, rather than a malignant one. Her conclusion was that Steven's tumour was a benign disease," Angelo concluded.

Maybe this was a benign disease, or maybe it had been malignant and God had changed the cells. I don't know. Doctors, as scientists, look at things and interpret what they are seeing. That first day, under the microscope, they saw cancer cells. Five days later, this new pathologist had seen cells that were a variation of normal cells from the same tumour.

By being willing to firmly state that she thought Steven's tumour was benign, this pathologist was the only person to give us a breath of hope and the strength to stay true to our convictions, and not suggest that we waiver from our decision to hold off on the chemotherapy. It was a very tough thing for a junior pathologist not to fall into line with her more senior colleagues. It actually could have been a career-altering decision, but her professionalism and integrity shone through. We had prayed for discrepancy and we got it. We knew God was there with us throughout everything.

Based on the new discrepancy, we were more confident saying that we would postpone or delay chemotherapy until circumstances changed that opinion. However, because of this major discrepancy, we decided to seek the opinions of other pathologists outside of our community, as perhaps there were too many issues starting to cloud a proper diagnosis. Three specialists from other hospitals entertained the possibility that Steven's tumour could be a benign disease, as well. Now, we definitely had discrepancy. Because of this, we decided it was time to take Steven home and try to get back to some semblance of normalcy. If something further were to develop we would deal with it then.

There were still some clinicians at the original hospital who insisted that Steven had cancer and still thought that he should be treated with chemotherapy. In some of their minds, there were concerns that we, as his parents, were obviously not thinking clearly and not accepting reasonable medical advice. We were told that some felt that entertaining a belief that Steven had a benign disease, and refusing chemotherapy, were serious errors in judgment.

Prior to taking Steven home, more than a week after he had been admitted, we asked his doctors to remove the Hickman catheter from Steven's chest. In our opinion, Steven was not going to have chemotherapy at this time. We were repeatedly told that it had to stay in, in case things got worse and treatment had to be started.

After two weeks of this discussion, during which time Steven was rapidly improving at home, we continued to insist that the catheter be removed. We knew that the specialists at the hospital were still waiting for Steven to get worse. They just could not believe that after all that had happened we were just going to take this child home with no treatment, whatsoever. They were waiting for Steven to get sicker and for more tumours to appear. We allowed them to continue to do numerous X-rays on him to detect signs of spread and growth.

During the third week, Richard called on Steven's oncologist and emphatically stated, "The tube comes out now!"

"We'll see about it next week," the oncologist said, humouring Richard more than taking his request seriously.

Richard replied by saying, "It will be out tomorrow, or you're going to have a lawsuit on your hands." Against what they felt was their better judgment, the catheter tube into Steven's heart was taken out. The surgeon adamantly informed us that he did not support our beliefs but would comply with our request.

Many times over the weeks, we had been told that our son was going to die. The doctors insisted that he needed chemotherapy and that we, his parents, were going to kill him by refusing the treatment. However, everything we had prayed for happened, and everything they had told us changed. Was this a healing? After we took Steven home, he continued to get healthier and healthier. It was inexplicable. It just happened. We did not question it.

◊ ◊ ◊

Over the next ten years, each Christmas, Richard sent a bouquet of flowers or a fruit basket to the female pathologist who had been the first to give us true hope. He thanked her for her professional and personal strength and for saying what she believed, in spite of the experts around her. She was a catalyst for the confidence in the continued discrepancies that allowed us to avoid the chemotherapy.

We believed that her findings were another answer to our prayers, enabling us to take our child home. We were able to have faith in his recovery and renewed hope in the future, believing that the disease would not return.

CHAPTER SEVEN

Going Home
 – Encircled in Love

Once we were home, in familiar surroundings and with all of us under one roof, Steven kept getting better–day after day, and week after week. By the end of the first week, the lump in his neck had gone down, until nothing at all could be noticed. In the back of our minds, we hoped that we had done the right thing. As Steven's health continued to improve, we were certain that we had indeed done the right thing. We were aware that to be 100 percent certain we had to wait a year, and then we would have to wait another five years to ensure remission.

We were very grateful. We were grateful for all of the continued prayers and grateful to the people who said, "When God heals, He does not take the healing back." We still desperately needed the prayers and the support of those around us. We wanted people to keep praying for Steven–to pray for his continued good health and total recovery.

◊ ◊ ◊

Taking care of Steven and our family consumed me. I read books on nutrition and made sure that we were eating the right foods to make us all healthy. I read spiritual books, looking for a sense of understanding of what had happened. I wanted to make sure that we were all recovering, both emotionally and physically.

A terminal illness, or even the threat of a terminal illness, affects everyone in the family. I learned that it is important to deal with not only the physical but also the emotional and spiritual well-being of everyone touched by an illness.

I remained home from work for two years, engrossed in ensuring that we were all well. During this time, I continued to pray: prayers of thanksgiving and prayers of gratitude. The books I read and the spiritual people who came into my life at that time told me that I had to pray with gratitude for what I needed. When God is thanked with sincere expectation, what is asked for will be received. Prayer became an integral part of my life. I knew, firsthand, that God was not to be called on only in times of great stress and dire need.

◊ ◊ ◊

About a month after Steven came home, he woke up one morning with a very high fever. "Oh, no!" I thought. Doubt of Steven's health began to surface. "Pray with me, Steven," I said, after giving him some medicine as I started to pray:

This is a house of God.
No one is allowed into this house, no evil forces.

We really got into some powerful prayer. I felt that I had a fight on my hands, and I had to protect my son from any unseen evil forces present. I was like a mother bear ready to protect her cub. I was encircling him with prayer and the power of God. The only thing I knew that could help him were the prayers. Suddenly, something came over me. I knew that negative forces were trying one more time. "No, you are not allowed to enter our lives and prey on our fears," I called out.

There is nothing more powerful than a mother's prayer for her child: she is filled with a total love and a fearless heart, and she will not waiver from her conviction.

That night, when Richard arrived home from his office, Steven said to him, "Dad, Mommy and I prayed this morning that the devil wasn't allowed in this house."

"You did?" Richard replied, looking at me out of the corner of his eye.

"Yeah, we did!" I responded.

Richard smiled. "Does that mean that I have to leave?"

Steven described the morning's event. "It's alright, Daddy. We prayed and I don't have my fever anymore."

I explained the whole situation to Richard. He understood my fears and was glad that the medicine I gave Steven worked. We knew that if the fever had not broken, we would have had to go back to the hospital.

◊ ◊ ◊

We are not the type of people to preach. Our intent is to simply share our experience. We lived it. We were there. We saw what we saw, and we truly believe that God was there with us, all the way through.

I feel that whatever happened with Steven was a miracle. There was a ripple effect. People spread the word. There were people praying for us from all over. There were people who had lost their faith and had not prayed in a long time. They were praying for us and recovering their own faith. There were people of other denominations and beliefs who prayed for us. Regardless of whom they were praying to, it made a difference. Steven was healed.

Good friends from our church and in our community talked about how the small community of Ancaster, Ontario, came together to pray for us. Our community rallied together for a common purpose. Calls were made for prayer from family to family, many with small children like ours. Parents stopped and hugged their kids, appreciated them a little bit more, and showed their love. I was told that the act of requesting prayer had a ripple effect throughout our town causing people to respond. Because we asked, they did it. It is true: "Ask and you shall receive."

Neighbours, friends, and family constantly brought food to the house and rallied around us during our time of need. Co-workers kept the medical practice going for Richard so that we could devote our energies to being with Steven. It was like we were all on a mission to pull Steven through.

◊ ◊ ◊

Once Steven came home, we had a big celebration. The house was filled with friends and family and feelings of great joy and relief. We celebrated our family bond, our faith, and our life. We did what we could to make sure our lives got back to normal.

The following March break, about six weeks after Steven's hospital stay, we all went to Disney World in Florida. The kids loved it. With us were my mother and two sisters, Aunt Diane and Aunt Jacqueline. When we had needed them, they came to our aid immediately. Now, we wanted them to be a part of this celebration.

I can not say for sure exactly what happened, and I will never know until I get to heaven and ask God myself. Our family believes that God was with us and that there was divine help. We felt it. We felt the strength of the prayers. We felt that we were being lifted up. We were given "moments of knowing" that Steven would be alright. It was like God was speaking directly into our hearts—giving us peace of mind while we walked through the darkness and lived with our fears. Although we were not able to eat or get proper sleep during Steven's hospitalization, we were given the strength to carry on.

From the very first day of Steven's ordeal, I was compelled to read the Bible. Every time I was home, I sought answers and felt that I had to go to God. I opened the Bible and would simply read it. It was what I was supposed to read and what I needed to read. Night after night, the Bible would open to the same page and I would read the following:

At that time you won't need to ask me for anything, for you can go directly to the Father and ask Him, and He will give you what you ask for because you use my name. Ask, using my name, and you will receive, and your cup of joy will overflow.

John 16:23-24

I knew that if I truly believed the words, they would come true. The words came alive to me and I *knew* that if I asked God to heal Steven, then He would heal Steven. The belief I had in my heart was strong and sincere and so powerful for me. I also seemed to be saying what I was supposed to say, and I know God was right there guiding me. He guided my prayers and he guided my words of comfort. The poem "Footprints" by Margaret Fishback Powers explains this so well: we don't see our footprints because the Lord carries us during our lowest times. That is exactly what He did for us. I know God was there, carrying us through.

On occasion, doctors in the hospital would stop Richard to ask if what they heard about Steven was true. "Has your son really been healed?" they would ask.

Many colleagues wanted to believe, but their sceptical scientific side would often cause them to add, "Well, I kind of believe it, but don't tell anyone else because they're going to think you're crazy." A number of doctors warned Richard that he should keep low-key about what happened. They understood his need to believe and agreed that unexplained things did happen, but they stood firm that he should be careful not to label it a miracle.

I am aware that people thought our family was a little off-the-wall when we started applying our spiritual beliefs to the material world. I have no problem with their scepticism, but I know what I know. Unfortunately, Richard had to take the brunt of it.

◊ ◊ ◊

Many times, physicians who did not know the outcome of our story, but knew that Steven had been ill, asked of his current condition:

"He's fine," Richard would say.

"Is he finished his chemo?" they would ask.

"He never had chemo," Richard would answer, knowing exactly what was going to be said next.

"I heard he had a neuroblastoma," was the most common reply.

Richard would then respond, "Yes, that is what all of the specialists thought."

Many often asked if Steven was really alright. Many asked why Richard eluded that something other than the medical establishment helped his son.

To this, Richard would say, "I don't know. Do you want to come and meet my son? You know, he seems fine."

Richard once had a pediatric psychiatrist stop him in the hospital. "I heard about your son. Tell me about him," the psychiatrist said. Richard recounted the story, only to hear a familiar warning: "I hope you're not telling too many people about that. They might think you're crazy. You have to go quietly, tell the few people you know, but the rest are going to think you're nuts." He added, "I tend to believe you, Richard, but people who don't know you, won't."

Richard added, "I have heard other doctors say the same thing. I have had lots and lots of people tell me that I should not be talking about this. They say that quite obviously the doctors made a wrong diagnosis, and maybe they did. Even if they did, and the possibility exists, the point is that it was our faith that got us through it. That was the thing–I can't imagine not having had our faith."

◊ ◊ ◊

In the retelling of Steven's story, when all of the facts of the case come out, there are usually one of two reactions: the story is either met with belief, or it is met with a measure of scepticism. Miracles in medicine are seen as being rare, and, to many, non-existent.

However, to us there was a miracle. After only a few months, my mother reached out and caught Steven's arm and felt that he seemed much stronger; so much so, that she remarked about it to us.

One year after the lump was found on Steven's neck, or son looked like a healthy eight-year-old. At the five-year mark, at thirteen years old, Steven was a strapping, healthy young boy and was involved in every sport imaginable. He was a walking image of good health, with no sign of recurrence.

ur Perspectives

CHAPTER EIGHT

uestions:

      I'm sure you have some.

I hope that by sharing the questions Richard and I have frequently been asked over the years that our story becomes a bit clearer. The following questions are answered by us Karen and Richard Zizzo, Steven's parents.

Question: The neuroblastoma, is it typical for it to come up that fast?

Answer: No, it is not typical for tumours to grow that quickly. The doctors also entertained the possibility of cat scratch fever, mononucleosis, and even atypical mononucleosis.

Question: Was it a lymph node in the neck that first appeared?

Answer: Yes, it was a lymph node. After being examined, the biopsy of the node indicated the presence of cancer cells. These were seen microscopically. The tumour was the size of a small orange, sticking right out on one side of Steven's neck. It was hard to believe how rapidly it came up. When it initially appeared, I thought it was a vascular lesion of some sort; and by playing hockey, he had damaged something there and was getting some swelling. But it was a solid tumour. It had no bruises over it, indicating that Steven hadn't been hit hard. Listening with the stethoscope, the tumour had no noises and the vascular system seemed fine. When I gave Steven the once over, he looked fine.

I later remember asking one of Steven's pediatric oncologists, "What do you think happened? Did my son have cancer? The child that you saw before the operation, did he have cancer?"

In reply, my colleague said that Steven's white blood cell count was normal and that he had no atypical lymphocytes. The oncologist said that Steven looked a little pale and skinny, indicating that it was probably not a viral infection, but it more likely was cancer. I realized that Steven *did* look pale, compared to how I was used to seeing him; but at the time, I thought that he looked normal. In retrospect, he had been quite pale for a while.

Question: Was there any itchiness associated with Steven's illness? I ask that because there is sometimes a generalized itch common with certain solid tumours of the lymph system. (This question was asked by a medical professional.)

Answer: Steven did complain of a generalized itch for some time before the lump on his neck appeared. We thought it might have been related to using a particular laundry detergent, or his not rinsing well enough after his daily shower. At the time, I was unaware of the relationship between itchiness and solid tumours of the lymph system.

Question: Were there any other intermediate lymph nodes?

Answer: Steven's doctors thought there were a few others under his armpit.

Question: But nothing specific?

Answer: The doctors did a lymphangiogram, a bone marrow aspiration, blood tests, CAT scans of his abdomen and brain, and an intravenous pyelogram. They found nothing else wrong. The growth in his chest did not appear to be in the lymph system. It was a big tumour that was very close to the spine. The doctors thought it was a neuroblastoma rising from the spinal cord and not a lymphoma. A day or two before the chest surgery, when comparing it to the growth on his neck, the doctors speculated that it could be a lymphoma. They felt certain that the chest tumour was the same disease that was in his neck. The doctors believed that there was a connection between the neck tumour and the chest tumour. They certainly were not entertaining the possibility of these tumours being totally independent of each other.

Question: Did you say Steven's chest tumour was on the left side of the lung?

Answer: There was a tumour on the right side of the neck and another tumour on the left side of the chest.

Question: If Steven had been treated with chemotherapy, what would his chances have been?

Answer: He would have become a statistic. One way or another, he would have been a statistic. We were told that some children have died with the first dose of chemotherapy. I was not prepared to take that risk. Once you begin chemotherapy, you are obliged to finish the course of treatment. In this case we were talking about a three-year course. We had a great deal of difficulty envisioning Steven, a lean seven-year-old to begin with, completing three full years of chemotherapy. We were afraid that his little body would not hold up.

As we prayed the morning after the conference with the doctors, it became apparent that we would have to do what we could live with. We had to weigh all of the possibilities, face the consequences of our decisions, and pray for guidance. We did not sleep much.

The first day we saw the oncologist, he confidently told us that "children in [Steven's] position have a 4% chance of surviving one year of chemotherapy, and realistically he has no chance." This oncologist believed that the two tumours were identical–that they had to be–and that the sooner we accepted Steven's fate, the sooner we would be able to deal with his inevitable death.

We would like to point out that this is an experience we had with an individual. This is not reflective of the entire medical profession.

Question: If Richard had not been a physician and still refused chemotherapy, what would have happened to your child?

Answer: We don't want to think about it. A lady stopped Richard in the hospital recently. She was a ward clerk. Three years prior to our son's problem, her grandson faced a similar situation. She had heard Richard say that the physician was a negative force who didn't treat people very nicely if they disagreed with him. She said that her family had dealt with a negative physician, as well. The doctor also suggested that this boy have chemotherapy. He died from the chemotherapy. When the autopsy results came in, it indicated that no cancer was found in the boy's body. Either the chemotherapy killed the cancer, or the chemotherapy killed the boy. Possibly, the chemotherapy killed them both. Richard was aware that such things happen. As a result, our decision had to be something that we could live with. A poignant piece of advice would be to get more than one opinion. Listen to the medical advice, but ultimately you will have to make your own decision.

We couldn't live with administering chemotherapy and that very treatment causing Steven's death. We would have dealt with it if it had happened, but that is not something we wanted to think about.

Question: Do you believe that a miracle or something resembling a miracle took place?

Answer: This is a matter that gets discussed often with believers and sceptics alike. The true miracle was the miracle of the ripple effect of the prayers. Many people prayed who did not normally pray. Many people thought about important aspects of their lives not often thought about: things like showing love to each other; hugging their children; being grateful for the little things in life; and finding pleasure in everyday activities.

Even Steven's doctors were forced to question the role of God in healing. Many issues surfaced. It was mind-boggling. We now feel that the miracle was not just for us; the miracle was for everyone around us, and we have to share our story.

Question: If people pray properly, do they have their prayers answered the way they want them answered?

Answer: We believe that the Lord knows what is good for us and what is not. He knows what we need to learn and what road we still need to travel. The first night that Richard and I prayed, we prayed that whatever God wanted, we would live with. We hoped that He wanted the same thing as we wanted—to save and heal Steven. Yet, no matter what, we would not forsake God but continue to ask Him to walk with us. Even if it was God's will to take Steven, we would continue to praise God and thank Him for the time we had with our son. We prayed for more time, if it was His will.

Up until Steven's illness, Richard and I did not pray that way. In the past we had prayed for our wishes to be granted. The circumstances of this event were so frightening. We knew that we could lose Steven. We were willing to place the outcome in God's hands. We did pray for Steven to be healed, and we told people that we would get through everything, no matter what the outcome, because God was with us. Many people responded sceptically. But we know that God really was with us.

After hearing of our help from God, people came up to us and asked why that when they prayed for someone to be healed, God didn't hear their prayers and help them as they asked. "Why did He answer your prayers?" was a question they often asked.

The only way I can respond is to say, "I don't know." I can't answer that. I think that when we accept God's will, we take the limits off God, thereby allowing Him to do the impossible.

Question: How is prayer able to hold such importance when one is inclined to be literally mad with rage at the tragedy for a child?

One, I would think, would be so incensed with anger that it would be difficult to imagine turning to God in prayer rather than in anger.

Answer: To the extreme, I heard someone relate the story about a mother who had come upon her son who had just been stabbed. As she prayed to God over his almost lifeless body, she said, "Thank you for giving me my son and for the years that we had together." We prayed that we could hold on to the memories of our life with Steven:

Thank you, thank you, Lord of all creation, for the joyful time we have had with your gift, Steven.
We are grateful.
We will take what we can get.
If it is another week, we will take it.

That is precisely the type of prayer said by the mother of the stabbing victim, and her son's life was saved. She said it was because she praised God for the gift of her son. It made her so happy that she at least had her son up until that time.

Perhaps that is a perfect type of prayer. Our gratefulness precipitated spontaneous prayer directly from our hearts. It was a natural loving act to pray this way for our child. And perhaps the "peace" we hear about so frequently from those approaching death has something to do with the acceptance and thankfulness in the Lord. Perhaps this is the true peace for which we are all searching.

At first, we did not want to share our personal story because it was difficult to expose our lives. People would look at us like we were crazy; yet we were given this experience and we have to share it. We have to talk about it. We have to give *hope* to other people. We have to show others how God works and how He worked in our lives.

CHAPTER NINE

C hanging Attitudes

On May 6, 1998, eleven years after Steven's recovery, I interviewed Father Con O'Mahoney. He had been our parish priest at the time of Steven's ordeal. I asked him for his interpretation of what he thought had happened: Was it a miracle? Did he believe in miracles? Did the experience have an impact on him or on the parish at which he was serving at the time?

Father Con replied that at the time he had been a young priest, only having been ordained for four years. It was his first full year at St. Ann's Parish in Ancaster, Ontario. At that time, he did not know if he had ever seen a miracle.

He told me that during our ordeal, he certainly saw a miracle in the amount of prayers sent out for Steven and in the distance the prayers had travelled. It was also a miracle in that the ordeal touched the people in the community and spread out into the wider environs. People's eyes were opened to the preciousness of their own healthy children, something that they had taken for granted on a daily basis. Furthermore, everyone witnessed the power of combined prayer. The end result was that people witnessed something extraordinary and, in witnessing it, it reaffirmed their faith.

Through the years, Father Con had witnessed the lives of many people radically changed through prayer. At our interview, he claimed, "Today, if you asked me if I believed in miracles, I would have to say, 'Yes.' My eyes have been opened to some of the changes that I have witnessed over the years."

Father Con recalls walking into the hospital and arriving just as our family was to begin a prayer. "I recall being asked to come to the hospital to minister to the Zizzo family, upon Steven being admitted. When I arrived, I entered a lounge area where [Richard and Karen] and many members of the family were gathered. As soon as I arrived, I was asked to lead the family in prayer. I was conscious of something in the air of the room. I can best describe it as "faith." There was a reverence. As I began to lead the prayer, each member of the family earnestly prayed every word with me."

During our interview, Father Con admitted that both the School Board Religion Consultant and the Hospital Chaplain had told him that as our family's Spiritual Director, his job was to make us face the gravity of our child's illness. He has been encouraged to help us accept it, and aid us while we entered the stages of grief.

However, once he witnessed the family asking for God's healing prayer to help their son, he could not give us a "reality check." He could not tell us that there was more of a likelihood that Steven would die than being healed. Upon seeing us, he could say nothing. He could only contribute his and the community's prayers for healing as we had requested.

Father Con O'Mahoney explained that he felt that his work with us that night was the beginning for him: of being allowed as clergy, to enter hospitals and play a more significant role in the healing process. Clergy are now allowed to be part of the team in the overall well-being of a patient. The clergy is recognized as the third part of the body-mind-spirit triad. The doors began to open for clergy to administer spiritually shortly after our experience.

Father O'Mahoney also talked about Steven's school. "We were preparing Steven's grade two class for First Communion, which was always a community event. The concerns of the church pastor, the grade two teacher, and Father Con, was the possibility of preparing these seven-year-olds for a classmate's funeral, soon to be followed by their own joyous First Communion. It was very dramatic, this range of emotions. Steven's grade two teacher began to deal with the children's feelings regarding their seriously ill classmate shortly after Steven had been admitted to the hospital. She had them draw pictures and write stories to send to Steven in the hospital. They sent letters, poems, and pictures of their prayers and thoughts for him."

Then Father Con painted a heart-warming picture, "In May of 1987, all of the grade two class, including Steven, celebrated their First Communion. It was a hugely emotional experience. It was the celebration of a mystery that could not be explained. Obviously, the children were receiving the body of Christ for the first time, and that was marvellous in itself; but there was also the celebration of Steven's new chance at life. There was not a dry eye in the church, especially from the Zizzo family. In all my years, and in all the parishes in which I served, I still remember Steven's ordeal as an unexplained mystery."

Not only was Father Con a witness to change, there were many other changing attitudes. During our time at the hospital, Richard and I broke a few rules. We brought in food that Steven liked so that he would eat and stay happy. Friends and family brought in video games, toys, and special books for Steven. These were things that made his stay more bearable and gave him a semblance of normality. We even brought in a clown to entertain him and take his mind off the procedures. Laughter is supposed to be the best medicine, and we were willing to try anything and everything.

Richard and I wore the same red sweaters every day so that the time in hospital would not seem so long to Steven. Richard felt that wearing the same bright red sweater would seem familiar and be a constant, comforting presence for Steven. I gladly washed it and had it ready for the next day. Richard believed in what he was doing, and I believed in him.

Richard and I were willing to do anything to help Steven. This included surrounding him with positive people and the things he enjoyed and loved. We even kept loved ones away until they could come into the room smiling, not crying. We were both there every day and made sure that Steven knew we were there for him. We made his healing a project or a mission. We had to support our son and handle the situation in the best possible way, regardless of the outcome. We pulled on every atom of our beings. We searched our minds to find everything that could help us in this quest and, hopefully, heal our son.

We had decided that we would not allow ourselves to think negatively. We would not accept the worst possible outcome. We would cross each bridge as necessary. We would keep our focus on the possible positive outcome and make it happen. This was our mission.

There has been a shift among the medical profession and mainstream society as well. Many doctors have begun to acknowledge that there could be more to health than blood cell counts and diagnostic tests and more to healing than pills and surgery. It is much more apparent that people, both medical and mainstream, are examining the connection between healing and spirituality. This change in attitude reflects the public's need for a more personal and, perhaps, spiritual approach to health and healing. Western medicine is high-technology medicine, which works the best in crisis situations. We can all agree that repairs to broken bones, the replacing of a heart, or bypass surgery require this high-tech medical care. Yet, increasingly, the stressful lifestyles that we are all a part of in the twenty-first century has led to many chronic illnesses. Approximately 70% of visits to doctors' offices are in the mind-body, stress-related realm. Because traditional modes of therapy such as pharmaceutical and surgical do not work well in all cases, many individuals seek solace in alternative therapies. For the first time since the discovery of the miracle cures of traditional Western medicine, we are beginning to see an appealing blend of Western medicine and of spirituality.

A 1995 study at Dartmouth University Medical Centre indicated that one of the greater predictors of survival after having open-heart surgery was the strength and comfort that patients' sought in their religious faith. (*Time Magazine*: Faith and Healing, Vol. 147, No. 26, Claudia Wallace, June 24, 1996, 34-40)

Today, the medical system is open to the idea of the mind-body-soul connection and regardless of what faith people may practice, they are allowed to make it part of their treatment. As long as the hospital can follow their medical protocol, the doctors and nurses are more open to the families' wishes.

*There are mistakes,
there are miracles,
and there is the power of prayer.*

Our Perspectives

CHAPTER TEN

*9*mpact on the Family

The two weeks that Steven was in the hospital, the months of recovery, and the emotional experience of living through the fear of Steven's terminal diagnosis impacted our lives forever, both physically and emotionally.

In an instant, Steven went from being a healthy seven-year-old to a sick boy with three months to live. To this day, the scars incurred during his procedures and surgeries are still visible when he has his shirt off.

Laura and Ryan, Steven's younger siblings, experienced the immediate absence of their parents and brother and care the of their grandmother and aunt. Although they were only five and two, respectively, they later said that they knew that something was wrong in the house.

Richard and I experienced a roller coaster of emotions. The relationship between us was strengthened through our commitment to our son and our faith in God. The relationship we had with our extended family was also strengthened. We had the prayers, support, and love of so many. They came to us when we needed them. For that, we will always be grateful.

I was a mother of three small children, had a Master's Degree in Social Sciences, and held a teaching position at a community college, which I had worked so hard to attain. For my son, I was willing to put that career on hold. I had asked for a leave of absence from my teaching position, but later changed that to a resignation. It was a very difficult thing to do, but my I knew that I would be able to pick up my career later, especially if I was doing the right thing for the right reasons.

Although I returned to a different career after staying home with the children for two years, my focus remained on the health and well-being of my family. I realized that my children would only be young for a short period of time. I did not choose a nine to five position; instead, I chose to open my own retail business. Although it was not less work or fewer hours, it gave me the flexibility to be available for my family. I hired people to be at the store when I needed to be with my children. I could greet my children at the bus and be at home to hear their stories at the end of the day. We could eat supper together, and I could take them to all of their swimming, music, and dance lessons. I could attend their sports events and school functions.

I did not just do this for them; I did it for me, too. Having nearly lost our son, I realized that there was a short window of time to be with the children. At the end of my life, I did not want to experience the weight of guilt or the sadness of regrets from making the wrong choices for me.

Laura and Ryan feel that the experience had a powerful effect on their lives, as well. Obviously, they witnessed the trauma surrounding their older brother. Their maternal grandmother and Aunt Diane moved into the house to take care of them while Richard and I were at the hospital.

Children feel the tension and fear of the adults around them, and I am sure that Laura and Ryan sensed the seriousness of what was going on, although the events occurring with Steven were never discussed with them. They were told that Steven was sick and that he had to stay in the hospital. We explained to them that Mommy and Daddy had to be at the hospital for Steven.

Laura and Ryan were very much a part of the family's prayers and discussions surrounding the happenings at that time. When people prayed for Steven, they also prayed for Laura and Ryan. They prayed for our family as a whole. That was what we needed to get through.

As a result of the ordeal with Steven, Laura and Ryan appreciate life more than most people their age. They have also always showed maturity beyond their years. They both recognized and freely voiced the value of prayer and faith very early on.

"You have to believe in the power of prayer, not just hope that prayer will work," both reiterated when asked questions about their brother.

◊ ◊ ◊

Laura

Laura, now twenty-two, sat down with me to discuss the impact of our family's trial on her. She remembers a great sense of the whole family coming together, including the extended family. There was sadness, and yet, an overwhelming love that radiated from both sides of the family. There was also the incredible concern shown by the parents and teachers at her school. Our community reached out to every one of us.

Laura recalls going to the hospital and playing in the waiting room and hallways, close to Steven's room. She was only allowed into Steven's room once he began to get better. Her visits with him did not happen often because of the complexity and urgency of his situation and because he came home so soon after the healing began.

It was to the relief of Richard and I that she said that she did not feel pushed aside. Our family rallied around her and Ryan. Richard and I still were present as much as we could be while caring for Steven, but she certainly knew that the concern of the adults had to be elsewhere. Steven was the most important concern at the time. The focus had to be on Steven in order to help him get better. She was aware that Steven was really, really sick and knew that he needed us. Laura knew that the family members taking care of her and Ryan loved them very much and did what they could to make sure she and her younger brother knew it.

Laura remembered how Richard and I would take turns coming home, one night to the next. During this time, she and Ryan were allowed to sleep in our bed with us. This was a real treat, as we normally did not allow this practice. Richard and I did what we could to maintain closeness with Laura and Ryan. We made sure that they knew that we were still present and accessible.

Laura believes that people have power in their lives. A person can choose how to react to situations. A person can choose to accept and fight for what they believe in, regardless of what the experts say–decide on what needs to be done, commit to it, and go for it. "Believing that you can do things, and having a positive attitude, will get you where you want to go. You have to act on your desires, not just pray for them." This motto continued to be important to Richard during Steven's illness. As our children got older, we continued to encourage them to live by the same.

◊ ◊ ◊

Ryan

Ryan was only two years old when Steven was in the hospital. At the age of nineteen, he talked to me about it. He felt that the whole experience with the family affected him greatly. He has a true belief in the power of family and the power of prayer.

The situation strengthened the family as a whole, and it created an attitude and desire to help others. Ryan willingly shares our family's story and openly calls it a miracle. He says that people his age accept what happened and say that it is amazing. In his own life, he is no longer afraid to try new things.

Knowing that his brother won the "battle" widened the parameters on what was possible. It removed barriers and limitations on what could be accomplished. Overall, Ryan believes that we need to have a positive attitude and focus on the odds that predict a positive outcome. He continues to help others and encourages them to achieve what they believe in. Ryan shares the experience because his family lived it and it might help others to believe. He has a strong sense of giving to others, of "paying it forward."

◊ ◊ ◊

Our extended family

All the lives of our extended family were affected by the experience as well. My mother, Joyce, was so incredibly supportive and always present for us. Mom remembers waiting with me outside the surgical suite when Steven's chest tumour was removed; she recalls the absolute euphoria when its removal proved to be benign rather than malignant as had been predicted. She feels that the power of prayer changed the outcome. She played a significant role in my emotional support and was my constant companion, praying by my side. She was a pillar of strength. Her strong belief in both the power of prayer and that Steven would get well helped give Richard and me the strength we needed.

My sister Diane moved right in, took care of the house, did the laundry, cared for Laura and Ryan, answered their questions, and tried to calm their fears. I did not have to worry about the other children or the home, with my sisters and all of our extended family helping out so generously. I especially remember the wonderful food supplied by Aunt Judy, our neighbour Josie, and many others during this time. The importance of this kind of support cannot be overstated.

My sisters and brother, Marc, along with all of Richard's brothers and his sister, our in-laws, and extended family remembered as we prayed in the Intensive Care Unit lounge that first night. They rallied in prayer, building a power and creating a force to give us strength.

Many others–including aunts and uncles, cousins and friends–were able to see the power of prayer, and for some it was an opportunity to witness and believe in miracles. My Aunts Carolyn and Clare spoke openly to us about how prayer was helping change the course of events for Steven. Over the years, we have seen many relatives turn to prayer in time of need. Because we were so open about the prayers and our requests for their prayers during Steven's illness, they are willing to discuss their prayers and share their experiences with us now. I especially remember Aunt Francine asking for prayer during the times her brother and mother were ill before they passed away. In our family, prayer proved to be a comfort and support.

◊ ◊ ◊

Aunt Ferne

I have an Aunt Ferne, whose spirituality was extremely strong as she prayed for us during our time of need. She completely believed that God could heal our son. She would say, "God has the ability and power to heal Steven. You must pray vehemently for his healing. What you ask of God, He will give you." She felt that she was being guided to pray for us. Aunt Ferne was not at the hospital with us, but she proved to be a "prayer warrior." A prayer warrior is someone whose purpose is to constantly pray for the people involved. "It is your experience, your journey, and your lesson to be learned," Aunt Ferne said.

When I asked her to speak of her experience during Steven's illness, she immediately brought up the incredible trust between Richard and Steven. She reminded me that the special bond between them had started at Steven's birth. When Steven was born, Rick came out of the delivery room crying. Aunt Ferne recalls being told by my mother that she at first thought they were tears of joy. Richard then anguished that although he was filled with joy, the tears were the result of an inexplicable and overwhelming sadness that we might lose Steven when he was young; that his life might be short.

As a result, Richard was motivated to bond and be extremely close to his son. It is now clear that this bond helped get Steven through the many ordeals of his sickness.

Aunt Ferne believes that the whole experience allowed our family to be witness to God's great glory: it was an opportunity to experience the power of prayer, His healing power, and ultimately His love.

◊ ◊ ◊

Our own family

Throughout the years, in our home, we openly discussed the "miracle" for Steven. Richard, myself, Steven, Laura, and Ryan have a strong sense of the power of prayer and it is a part of our everyday lives. We have an attitude of gratitude for the things in our lives. We value our time together and feel blessed for having been shown these lessons so early.

Every day, I personally thank God for the little things. Not for the material possessions but for the gift of family, of being together, and of loving each other. I have a strong love for people and appreciate everyone, regardless of their position or status in life. I find it difficult to tolerate the prejudices that are often evident in our world. The experience of Steven's illness opened my eyes. I am more aware of the value in everyone and the lessons that we can learn from each other.

I really understand now that a sense of family is the most important characteristic you can instill. Knowing that you are there for each other and rallying together in your love for your family members creates a common goal. The combined prayers and love results in an incredibly powerful force unlike any other.

I also learned that when things are too big for you, it is alright to ask for help from your family, your friends, and, especially, from God. Everyone is happy to help, and it is a gift that you give to them: letting them help. When our family allowed ourselves to ask for help, we were overwhelmed by much love and support from others.

CHAPTER ELEVEN

Steven's Reflections

When asked about his thoughts, Steven provided the following insights:

I only understood that I was sick. I did not understand the severity of what was happening. Dying was not an option that occurred to me. It didn't enter my mind. As a seven-year-old, I had never heard the word "cancer" applied to me. The only other time I had been in the hospital as a patient was when I was five years old. I had to have my tonsils removed. There had been a bunch of needles that were painful. This time, they weren't doing that, so I didn't think I was sick.

I recall feeling sorry for the other children in the children's ward while I was there. They all seemed so much sicker that I. For instance, there was a boy with a broken foot who could not get out of his bed and had no toys with him. I remember sharing my toys with him. There was another boy who had to have dialysis every week, my dad explained to me. I felt horrible for him. I also saw a boy with a shaved head. I was told that he had a brain tumour and might die. But, I knew that I would get better. At the time, I thought more about the hockey practices and games that I was missing than being in the hospital.

◊ ◊ ◊

Having visited the hospital on so many occasions with my dad, I had no fear of what went on there. It was not a scary place to me. I knew that some people died, but they were really sick.

I wasn't sick. Both my father and uncle are doctors and I knew that doctors and nurses made people better. I was curious about everything, but not afraid. During all of the procedures, I trusted that the surgeons would do what they do, and that everything would be alright. Years later, I realized that this was the same trust witnessed in the eyes of many of my father's patients. They trusted and respected him and knew that everything would be fine.

There were two occasions that I remember being a little nervous. The first was when an uncle came to visit me at the hospital. He cried when he saw me and I couldn't understand why. I thought that someone should talk to him to explain that he had it all wrong; my problem wasn't that serious.

The second incident was when a nurse hooked me up to an IV. Suddenly, I was restricted. "Oh no! This means that I'm sick. Only people who are going to be in hospital for a while get these. I'm not going home right away!"

I don't remember being in pain during my hospital stay, but I do remember being a little anxious at times. During my surgery, before the anaesthetic kicked in, the doctors tilted me on my side. I thought that this was strange. I didn't think that people had surgery any other way than on their backs.

While I was in hospital, at least one of my parents was with me at all times. They were always there and never left me alone. Looking back, I know my parents made sacrifices for me. I thought it was pretty cool. I am so thankful.

The way I was raised prepared me for this experience. I had always been allowed to explore and had not been restricted from trying things. As a child, I didn't get away with poor behaviour; I had to suffer the consequences of my actions. I was given the freedom and trust to try things without letting it go too far. Because of this, I knew my parents would look after me for the time in the hospital, too, and that everything would be OK.

I remember that there was a lot of love around me in the hospital. The love came from family, friends, and acquaintances that visited. Many visitors snuck in food—just like the cookies and milk that were snuck in by the nurses at the hospital my dad did his rounds at. I loved this outlet to normalcy because I hated the hospital food. Aunt Clare brought me my favourite red gelatine dessert. Mrs. Craig brought macaroni and cheese meals. Both of these things were real treats for a seven-year-old boy who had been on intravenous foods.

I recall the things that cheered me up: Uncle Kevin brought me a King Kong movie and a Wrestlemania magazine; Uncle Allen brought me a wrestling ring and every wrestling figure available; Rob DiBacco, a next door neighbour who was like an older brother to me, brought me a car magazine knowing that cars were a real passion for me; and my Uncles Michael and Chuck visited often and made me laugh. My parents even brought in a clown to give me balloons. My class made me a special book for me with hand-drawn pictures and get-well wishes. It made me feel very special; I don't remember them doing that for anyone else. Angela, a special friend from my class said she couldn't find a gift to bring me so she gave me her own stuffed bear! I make no mistake about that bear, it was the nicest gift I received.

It seemed as though everyone was on a mission to find things to occupy my time. I was showered with gifts, visitors, love, and humour. Everyone came together to be with us. It really helped.

As soon as I was able, I wore my own special pyjamas and had my Charlie Brown and Snoopy pillowcase brought from home. I know now that our family broke a lot of rules to bring me the things they did, but the rules needed to be broken, and I'm glad that the hospitals have since changed and relaxed their protocol regarding the healing and emotional environment of a place trying to treat the ill.

◊ ◊ ◊

Steven's Reflections

My experience has taught me to keep perspective on events in my life. I appreciate things more. Although I have a lot of material things, I appreciate them, but don't take them for granted. I know that there is more to life than those things. I try not to sweat the small stuff—school, relationships, sports, money—and try to keep everything in perspective. I realize that living, or just being alive is important enough. Life is a gift that is taken for granted by most of us. I don't worry about things to the same extent as many of my peers. I feel I have been given maturity beyond my ears. Everyone is the same; we just don't look the same. When we sit with people whose body is disabled, we can learn from them. There is strength and wisdom that is developed from what they have gone through. My parents have said that I am more sensitive that other kids my age. They say that this is because I lived through what I did. If I was diagnosed correctly, I should not be here. Yet, I am. From this, I have learned that no one has the right to take away someone's hope.

I overcame odds and others can, too. I no longer question whether I can do something. I believe that you must make a commitment to go after things. When I was in grade ten, I knew that I could get into medical school. I knew that there would be a place for me.

Every thing happens for a reason. It's to prepare you for something ahead. It helps you be a better person. I feel that I am being called to be a part of the "helping professions" somehow, possibly in the area of alternative heather where the power of prayer has a place. Hopefully the gateway will be through studying medicine.

◊ ◊ ◊

I was raised in the Catholic Church and studied various religions. I came to understand that people need religion for strength. I don't think that one religion is right and another is wrong, but it is important to have something bigger than yourself to believe in. My parents' belief in their Catholic faith definitely gave them strength during the very trying time when I was in the hospital. I know that when I was sick, the doctors were doing their best work, but I believe that there was something bigger going on. I think that I am here for a reason. For me, that reason is to help people.

I am thankful for my life and realize that life is fragile. People die every day. It is out of our control. I think that I am living extra innings so I live life to the fullest. A good life should not be measured in the number of years, but in how you live those years.

The whole experience has taught me such incredible lessons. I now believe in the mind/body relationship. I promote the power of a positive attitude. When discussing this with someone, they seem to understand this concept better if they are religious or spiritual. I experienced this power firsthand and discuss it passionately. I know how fortunate I am to have the support, love, respect, and encouragement of my family.

I look at the world and want to tell people to do what is right for them, not necessarily always what is expected of them by others. I was raised to be an independent thinker and to take responsibility for my actions. It is not what others are doing that matters, it is what you do that truly counts.

I draw strength from God. I do pray sometimes, but I believe that there is a direct link to Him; He knows our thoughts, our needs, and hears our unspoken prayers. I have to believe in miracles and a higher power. What happened to me is hard to explain. Was it a misdiagnosis? Maybe. But the power and strength of the prayers said for me were present. Goodness came out of all of it.

◊ ◊ ◊

Over the years, I have often been asked by others to share my experience. The most frequently asked questions are: "Did you really have cancer?" and "Were you really going to die?" Many times I turned to my parents and other members of our family to if I really did have cancer, and if I was really supposed to die like the doctors said. The story was recounted as many times as I asked to hear it. After listening to the story one day, I asked my mother what she thought of it all.

She responded by saying that "the first day you were in the hospital, we were told that you had cancer. The tests and biopsy showed cancer cells. However, by the end of the first week, things had changed from terminal cancer, which equaled death, to a cancer that could be treated with chemotherapy. This change in prognosis gave you a chance at life. Something happened to me and to you, and to all of us. We can't explain it; we just know it happened. We took you home two weeks after being admitted."

I got healthier while at home. The lump on my neck disappeared. What exactly happened? For my parents, it was a miracle that occurred because of the power of prayer. Some people would like to explain the whole event away as a wrong diagnosis. But why were cancer cells seen and confirmed the first day in hospital? Did those cells change? Certainly the prayers for discrepancy came to fruition. With discrepancy came the realization that my parents were not prepared to subject me to three years of chemotherapy based on a continually changing situation—especially when the prognosis was changing for the better.

◊ ◊ ◊

Years later, when my mother was asked how this experience has affected me, she answered: "Steven certainly has been positively affected by this experience. We see that he is wise and mature beyond his years and able to cope with many things that rattle his peers. Both in grade school and high school Steven would help his classmates by encouraging them. He told them that they could do anything they set their mind to. We know that he truly believes

Our Perspectives

that if he can do it, they can too. He lived through a battle as a seven-year-old and has the battle scar to prove it. Steven knows how important it is to be kind and compassionate to people–all people. Steven has a sense of mortality, unlike many of his peers. He knows that all is precious and that life can change, or be taken away, in a minute."

◊ ◊ ◊

I remember the New Year's Eve after my hospitalization. My dad and I went to a hockey game in Buffalo, NY, and made sure that we were home before midnight so that we were with our family to ring in the New Year. When the clock stuck twelve, everyone in the room began to celebrate. I stepped away from the action and went to a private corner of the room to pray. I thanked God for the year our family had lived through and asked Him to watch over my family throughout 1988. It was a prayer of thanksgiving and gratefulness. Even at seven, I believed in the power of God and knew that He was right there with us all the time. I knew that He could help us when we needed it. We just needed to ask.

Prayer continues to be an important part of not only my life, but also everyone in my family.

◊ ◊ ◊

I have always had the attitude that "you can do anything you set your mind to," and "if you can't do it on your own, ask God and He will help you." I have seen examples in many instances. In talking to some of my friends who have said things like, "I can't do it," or "I can't do that," I often say, "What do you mean you can't do that? You can do anything!" The odds were against me. I feel that I have strength within me that has come directly from my childhood experience.

I have always tried to be sensitive and offer support to those others do not see as their equals. On one particular day, I came home from school and told my parents of a boy I had seen being teased by his classmates.

"When kids are making fun of someone, what should I do? How do I help him?" I asked.

"Well, why don't you befriend him?" my mother answered. I was raised with a Christian attitude towards others; an attitude that I try to share with other people.

The next day, I made an effort to talk to the boy. He was no different than any other kid at my school.

My experience continues to affect me emotionally, spiritually, and physically: I try to be the best person I can be and help those I can, I believe in the power of prayer, and I still have the scars of my biopsy and of my surgery. If I take my shirt off, the large scar on my back is very noticeable. When a person sees it for the first time, they usually ask about it. I believe that by answering their questions I can turn a negative experience into a positive one. It is a chance for me to share my story and help people believe.

CHAPTER TWELVE

Richard A. Zizzo, M.D. Comments

Richard speaks about the healing:

At the time, as a doctor, I did not know if a miracle happened, or if there was "a healing". As a father, I did believe that God healed Steven. I know that God helped my wife, my family, and me. I also know, without a doubt, that this experience had a positive effect on our family and showed us why we have faith. There was a positive impact on hundreds, and likely thousands, of people through the multiplier effect. It was because of our faith that we believed that healing and survival were possible. We believed in God; we believed He worked miracles. We still believe that He do these things.

When the capabilities of medicine were explained and clearly delineated, the prognosis was death in three to twelve months, likely closer to three, with or without treatment. We believed that God was with us. If this prognosis were to change, it would only be through the work of God. At that time, and even now, the concept of prayer as a viable addition to medical treatment was not popular. Praying was considered acceptable at the hospital but only as an adjunct to medical treatment. Actually expecting that through prayer you may get a remission in disease, or a healing, was considered improbable by many but impossible by most, and it fell in the domain of being a last resort. We asked everyone we knew, and those we did not, to put Steven in their prayers.

There were people who came to my office and told me

that they had prayed for Steven. There were prayer groups and churches that had heard of our situation and included him in their prayers. There were even a few doctors who asked if Steven could be included in the prayer group to which their wives belonged. I had no idea that these people had prayer groups going and that they were common. Support like that occurred and I found it heartwarming, as well as encouraging.

We asked a patient in my brother Angelo's medical practice, who is a pastor, to have his church pray for Steven. We were later told that the entire congregation rose to their feet and prayed. We asked a distant relative to ask his brother, a priest stationed in Rome, to pray for Steven as if the proximity to the Vatican and the Pope may have had a special benefit. Maybe it did. My brother David and sister Carolyn encouraged us to pray to Brother Andre from Montreal, who was being canonized as a saint at that time. I really believe that the focused prayer of thousands of people had a miraculous effect on the way this crisis turned out.

◊ ◊ ◊

There certainly is a spiritual part of my family practice. I am a physician; I deal with science. People come to me to get the science-based medical approach to their health needs. I am clear about that, just as my patients are; and that is what I give them. My licence to practice medicine requires that I live up to the standards of practice in my community. As any physician, I ensure that I meet those standards of good and competent care.

I chose to become a family physician because I wanted to treat the whole person in the context of their family and daily life. I felt that family medicine was the area of medicine where I could do that best. Sometimes, but not very often, I would receive requests from patients to pray with them. Previous to our experience with Steven, I could not bring myself to pray out loud with my patients so I said the prayers silently. But one patient in particular broke me of that insecurity. This was a wonderful, God-loving, older fellow who made "no bones" about his love and devotion to God. He had a ministry that he had developed later in his life and he spread it unabashedly.

When Steven was sick, this man was on vacation in Florida. There were two people I knew who I had to have pray for Steven: this man and Sister St. Brigid, a nun of the Sisters of St. Joseph convent. I managed to get a message to Florida, requesting that this gentleman pray for Steven. He not only prayed for Steven, but he got on a religious radio call-in show and put out a request for prayers for "Steven back in Ontario." After the outcome of Steven's illness had become known, this man's son, who did not follow his father's spiritual path at the time, turned around and started to walk firmly in the same path as his dad.

Many months later this dear older fellow died. I was away, so the non-Christian physician colleague who was taking care of my patients went to his apartment to do the pronunciation of death. When I returned, my colleague told me how impressed he was by the love that the family showed to this man and the strength they received from their Christian faith. It motivated my colleague to want to learn more about the Christian religion. When he told the grieving family, he was given a Bible. Even after his death, my patient's belief was that strong. His family knew that the right thing would be to encourage the doctor and give him the information he needed.

When my patient visited me in the months prior to his death, he requested that we take a few minutes during the visit to pray together. His prayers were not rote verbiage but were prayers constructed as he went along; and they always included the request that "God pour the precious blood of His son, Jesus" over the ones we love so that they could be healed by the suffering that took place on Calvary. I will always hold that passage very close to my heart. I felt a closeness to God with those prayers because we both, in very different ways, felt the emotional pain of a son suffering in physical pain.

I have suggested to many patients that they may need to extend their source of strength and recovery beyond the confines of the normal Western medical establishment. I do recommend acupuncture, physiotherapy, relaxation therapy, or whatever I feel would be a suitable adjunct to the conventional therapy that patients are receiving. I strive to give the best care available and am willing to look outside the norm for that. I am very cautious not to suggest, or imply, that they should discount traditional medical advice or practice. It would be contrary to the practice of medicine most commonly found in my community and, therefore, not acceptable.

Often I find myself dealing with patients dying of a terminal disease. In family medicine there are so many types of illness that affect patients and many emotions that come with knowing them thoughout their lives that a doctor must develop methods of handling the trauma that is experienced during times of physical and emotional distress. Not only do thses methods help patients and their families, but they can also help the doctor.

Sometimes I find it helpful to say to the patient, "Do you know that you are actually privileged because you know you are dying?" Some people do not accept my statement very well at first; so I must be cautious about how I say it, and follow with: "The way it stands at this point, you are going to die; but you can look at this and say, 'How am I going to deal with my death? How am I going to die?' Knowing the event is imminent allows for a certain degree of planning. Those who experience a sudden and unexpected death do not have this same opportunity." I continue this train of thought by explaining how I believe we have three areas to look after throughout our lives and especially when facing a terminal illness.

The following is how I would approach these areas, as a healthcare provider. This is my "Life Component Checklist":

1. There is the **Medical Component** to deal with. As a medical doctor and part of the healthcare team, I will provide the best treatment possible for each step of the illness. For pain control, dietary management, mobility issues, or other signs and symptoms of the illness, I am the "go-to guy". If you have got a problem, call me.

2. I call this second part the **Material Component**.This is the settling of your business and personal affairs; It involves your estate planning and Will, your mortgages and loans, your insurance, and even the funeral plans. Maybe there are other issues that need to be dealt with; this is the time to think about them. At the least I want my patients to be aware of the fact that they can take part in vitally important issues related to their death *prior* to their passing on. I use the term "passing on" because I believe they truly are doing just that. During this component, I also suggest that people say personal good-byes to their family and friends. We discuss all these issues in detail to determine if, and how, each may be a significant item for them.

3. There is the **Spiritual Component**. I do not know if it is the right order to put the spiritual as being third, but there are three components and the dying patient is going to have to deal with all of them, regardless of the order. I do not mind dealing with this issue; I find it very easy to do, even if the person does not believe in God. It is amazing that some people never consider this point until it is brought to their mind through this three-point checklist.

I thank God that I have this checklist. I wonder if it has brought anyone to a place they would never have been otherwise.

◊ ◊ ◊

The following is a verbatim statement I made. It was recorded during an engagement that Karen and I were asked to speak at about three years after Steven's recovery:

If I get asked to share the story of our son's healing, I have difficulty doing it, but I think that it's something that I have to do. As a physician and a scientist, I have to use caution when talking about miraculous healing because, when doing so, I am going against some of the principles inbred into the medical profession. Although it is not easy, I have to speak up. I don't want people coming to me thinking that I can miraculously heal their disease through prayer. If they want to pray, that is fine. I am open to that. I even ask people, on occasion, if they have "thought of God" in their life. I am comfortable with dealing with dying patients in terms of this type of palliative counselling. I still have difficulty discussing this personal family situation and sharing it publicly.

Seventeen years later, I have a willingness to discuss what happened and how I view the experience with Steven's illness. I have felt the pain of having a sick child. I know the pain of anticipating the death of a child. I still do not know the pain of losing a child, and certainly can not imagine the enormity of that; but as I deal with others who experience these things, I can more easily identify with their situation. I can be even more open and humane now that I have been where I have been and seen what I have seen.

I am not concerned that my reputation will be affected adversely if I suggest that people consider religion and faith in their lives. I have reintroduced people to their churches by bringing this void to their attention. Helping people be completely "well" includes the spiritual aspect in whatever way is important to that individual. Some people do not realize that they need an "Aspirin-a-day"; some people do not realize they need a "prayer-a-day." I just try to find out what people need to in order to maintain optimal health and give them the coordinates to steer in that direction.

The role of faith during our time of need was so important that it continues to be a vital part of my life and my practice now.

◊ ◊ ◊

I recently went over the Life Component Checklist with a patient with metastatic bowel cancer. She was entering the final stages of her disease. She had become very sober at her reality and made sure that each day had a special meaning. Her husband died prematurely many years earlier, and since then she had ignored her church and religion; maybe out of anger at God, maybe out of lack of interest. She was willing to reconsider the role of God in her life as it was coming to its earthly conclusion, but she was hesitant to take the first step. She thought her change in faith was unfair: that she was asking for his help now in her time of need, not having prayed to him for so many years.

After a conversation outlining what my thoughts were on her perspective, and with her acceptance, I referred her to the priest in her neighbourhood. I called the church office, gave a very brief reason why I was making the referral, and booked an appointment time in exactly the same way I would have if the patient needed a referral to a heart specialist. Only in this instance, I made the call myself and in the presence of the patient. I do not expect to receive a consultation note in return. What feedback I did get, however, was when the patient returned to me with a word of thanks and a hug. At the time of my writing this passage, she continues to see her priest, the cancer specialists, and me regularly.

When all else fails and things are bleak, and there is doubt as to where to turn, there is something very reassuring in knowing that God is there. I went to a Catholic high school and played on the football team. I remember so many times before a game, in the pre-game prayer, that we mentioned as a team that we knew God would be there with us on the field. Now, off the football field, I use that same belief to get his help when living my life. I am never alone and always have somethone extra on my side.

When the medication does not work, the psychotherapy is not completely successful, or the pain just will not quit, sharing our suffering and need with a power beyond us should be of added benefit. It often is. You may have to ask before you receive.

In 1988, a gentleman came into my office. Five years previous to this visit, he had a kidney removed because of cancer. He had symptoms of something going wrong in his stomach. We did the necessary tests and found out that he had cancer again. A biopsy was done and showed that it was the recurrence of the previous tumour. When the surgeon called, I was told that on the biopsy, they "found out that the patient has recurrent metastatic cancer and he is going to be dead in three to six months." The oncologist suggested that I call the patient and tell him the news.

Incredulously, I asked, "Give him a call and tell him *that?*"

"Yeah, that's the best way to deal with it," the surgeon responded. "Give the guy a call."

I gladly took the responsibility of passing on to the patient the information, but I knew that I would not do it the way the surgeon had suggested. I hung up and reflected on what I thought was his insensitivity. I could not imagine closing the doors of hope for a patient who had already been through a diagnosis of cancer once before. My receptionist called the patient and booked an appointment to see both him and his wife.

When they arrived, we sat down to discuss the situation. They knew it was serious.

"You have a problem," I began. "You know we did the biopsy, and now a diagnosis has been determined."

"What is it, doctor?" the patient asked

"Your cancer has come back," I said.

"How bad is it?" the patient's wife asked.

"It is very bad," I said, trying to be sensitive while being direct.

"How bad is 'very bad'?" he asked.

"There are two things we can do for you. First, there is only one thing we can do for your cancer and that is to cut it out. It is not the type that can be radiated, nor is it the type that you can give chemotherapy to. We are going to have to surgically remove what we can. We are pretty confident at this point that it is not totally resectable. From the tests that we did, we can see that it is so widespread that we will not be able to save your life medically. We suggest that an operation be done to bypass the area of cancer that is interfering with your bowel. This procedure will allow you to eat, bypass the obstruction, and digest your food."

"How long?" the patient asked.

"For what?" I replied.

His wife added, "... before he dies."

"No one knows exactly, but we do have educated guesses, estimates, and probabilities. I have been told three to six months."

The family stared in disbelief and I could only sit and let the news sink in for a few seconds, just long enough to be able to continue. "Second, the real reason I have you in here is to tell you that you have a disease that you have to handle. We can't cure this. You will have to cure this if it is to be done."

"What do you mean?" the patient's wife queried.

"Well, we, as medical people, can't cure everything. We don't know how to cure your illness, but maybe you can. Maybe there is something inside of you that will help cure this disease."

I told the couple about Steven. I told them that we had been given terrible news, but somehow he got better and survived. Maybe it was prayer, or maybe the doctors were all wrong from the beginning. But we were given a terrible prognosis and he still got better. I hoped the same would happen for this patient, but I did not know what this couple would have to do, if anything, to beat this.

"I know that prayer helps, and so does a positive attitude, humour, good thoughts, and getting rid of all the baggage you have been carrying around with you. Make your amends with people. Get things in order. Deal with it all. Maybe that will help," I said to prepare them.

He lived several years beyond the time that we prognosticated.

The patient came to my office for years after I told him and his wife about his cancer recurrence, for regular checkups. He said he just tried to be as positive about life as he could be and think of the good things instead of the bad. One day, when he came into the office looking sick, pale, thin, and weak, I inquired about his state. In response, he said, "I have cancer. I am supposed to look sick!" This was his way of adding humour to his situation.

Every three months I got an update from the cancer clinic for this patient. I loved it! Each letter said the same thing: "This man does remarkably well despite the lack of chemotherapy."

He and his wife continued to keep up their house for five years during his illness before moving into an apartment. One day, I asked if he had become religious since this event. He said, "No, I haven't."

"Really, I thought you would have," I replied.

"No, I didn't. I just say a prayer every night."

"When did you start doing that?"

"After I was in your office: every night, at least every night. Sometimes even a little bit more. Do you want to hear it?" He began reciting Psalm 23 as he was taught it:

The Lord is my Shepherd: I shall not want.

In verdant pastures he gives me repose;

Beside restful waters he leads me; he refreshes my soul.

He guides me in right paths for his name's sake.

Even though I walk in the dark valley I fear no evil;

for you are at my side

With your rod and your staff that give me courage.

You spread the table before me in the sight of my foes;

You anoint my head with oil; my cup overflows.

Only goodness and kindness follow me all the days of my life:

And I shall dwell in the house of the LORD

for years to come."

And then he said, "Oh, this is my little part that I add myself."
He continued to repeat for me his own conversation with God.

Not only was he saying a prayer every day, which he never did
before; but, also, he was saying it at least once a day. Plus, he
added a personal passage to it. I think he became religious.

◊ ◊ ◊

Similarly, a participant at a seminar on the "Power of Prayer in
Healing," shared the following story with us:

"I had cancer twenty-five years ago, and I had quite an experience
when I was in the hospital. At that time, my husband was into his
thirteenth year of Hodgkin's disease. I remember praying for him
at the time: 'Lord, I will accept him whatever way you leave him
to me.' My husband underwent radical surgery. He was thirty-one
at the time.

We had a ten-week-old son when I found out I had cancer. I was
devastated. The word troubled me more than the disease, and I
said to the Lord, 'I do not want to have the operation.' The doctor
said that he could not even guarantee me six more months of life.

I sat down, I cried, and I prayed. Then, I just felt this over-whelming strength embrace me. I made the decision to have the cancer surgery. While recuperating in the hospital, I kept walking up and down the corridor and prayed to the Lord, 'Just spare me until my son is educated and then if you want to take me, take me. But just let me be around until he is educated.' My son is now thirty-nine years old."

She continued, "My husband lived for twenty-one years with Hodgkin's disease. He died from other causes. I thank God over and over again for the emotional pain and suffering that I experi-enced. Through it, I came to know Him in such an intimate way. The pain became a blessing. The hurt became grace. I became so aware of how He cares."

$$\Diamond \ \Diamond \ \Diamond$$

At that same seminar another participant shared a similar story:

"The previous summer, I worked in a facility for physically handicapped children. There was a little fellow who was about the age of your son, seven or eight. His name was Steven, also, and I kind of took a shine to him because I have a son, Steven, who is fifteen. Little Steven had an astrocytoma, a serious type of brain tumour. He must have been in pain because he would lie down and then all of a sudden would scream.

Many months later, just by chance, and I think it was with the Lord's guidance, too, I happened to visit him as a healthcare worker. He had had surgery to remove the original brain tumour, but it returned and had to be removed again. Now, for the third time, it had metastasized in his brain. I visited with his mom, in their home, and I was overwhelmed by their acceptance. She told me that she gave him to the Lord the moment the first tumour came. 'If the Lord heals Steven, then I will be the first one to praise God, but if he chooses to take him, that is fine with me, too.' She was with him every moment. I couldn't help but wonder, as I stood there and watched this child, how many people had been touched by this beautiful gift that was Steven. Every nurse, and every physiotherapist involved in his case, agreed that he was a beautiful boy and he really was God's special gift.

I feel I had to say this. I think of my teenaged son, although he is not ill. I believe that with the faith shown here today by the people in this seminar and with the example of the mother who sits with her son, putting him in God's hands, that I could have the courage to do the same."

I remember another patient who came to my office shortly after our Steven was sick. He was a very big fellow and as nice as could be imagined. He really loved his wife and his family, and he had no hesitation telling people how important they were to him. He came to my office and I normally started with my routine questions: "Have you quit smoking yet?" "How's the diet going?" instead he said, "Doc, when I heard your son was sick, I got down on my knees and prayed to God. I haven't prayed on my knees in twenty years. I don't do that, but I did it for you and your son!" I started to cry. I thanked him.

This gentle man died several years later due to cancer. When it came time to prepare for his death, and when I got to the part where I discuss the Spiritual Component, he assured me that they already had that part well under control. I have never forgotten the day he died. Every year on that date I say a prayer for him. He prayed for my son and I will remember that always.

Another patient with a remarkable story was of a middle-aged woman with three brain tumours. She underwent "palliative radiotherapy" to decrease the size of the tumours. She and her family came to my office to discuss her problem, shortly after the radiotherapy. I quite frankly told them that a cure for her problem through conventional medical therapy was unlikely. I suggested that the best way of dealing with the problem was to attend to the issue of making her life a happy experience. I suggested that she use laughter therapeutically; have a "good clean living"; reduce emotional burdens by forgiving others for what they may have done to her in the past; do things to help others; and keep God in her life.

By living this way, she changed the course of things. I believe she treated herself by prayer and redirected her life in positive ways. She likely handled her illness through some sort of inner strength that she harnessed and applied and, I am told, she prayed. I have no other explanation except that some tumours behave differently than expected.

Possibly, prayer is part of what makes the difference. Prayer seems a viable addition to traditional treatment. I would not suggest to anyone to turn down traditional medical treatment or replace it with unproven therapies. My role here is to explain what I have seen and been through, biased as it may be. I will always take advantage of having an extra player on my team. I believe that I have seen prayer alter the course of disease.

These testimonies give strength to those of us who have challenging journeys, and they also enrich the lives of those sharing the stories and those who hear them.

So if you ask me today, "Was Steven's story a miracle?" I would answer, "definitely!" He had a medical problem that was seen by experts, a biopsy was done, and the diagnosis was made. The prognosis was terminal. Treatment was outlined but never initiated, except for the surgical part. He had the Hickman catheter inserted, and chemotherapy was planned but never took place. Twenty-two members of our family were there when the doctor told us the diagnosis and the prognosis; and then the priest walked in—and we prayed. And God answered. And Steven lives. And we realize how faith got us through an ordeal of a lifetime.

CHAPTER THIRTEEN

aren's Reflections & Lessons Learned

Years of reflection have crystallized my thoughts as they relate to the events of many years ago. I will share some of those reflections and the lessons we learned.

There is strong symbolism and parallelism between Richard taking Steven's hand during painful procedures, when Richard suggested that the pain could leave Steven and go into his dad's hand to be taken away, and God's promise to do the same. Is that not what our Lord offers us, too? He will take away all of our pain, suffering, illness, and emotional hurts. He will love and support us always. We need only ask Him, and He will be there for us.

I will not forget you. I have held you in the palm of my hand.

Isaiah 49:15-16

I also recall praying in Steven's hospital room that first night when he was admitted. We prayed "a prayer of surrender." We realized that we had no control. We surrendered the situation to God. Given the diagnosis that night, no one in the medical profession could save Steven's life. The prognosis was grave. There was nothing else we could do; there was nowhere else to turn.

When you fully surrender to God, He can work through you to make things happen. You must take your hands off, so that He can put his hands on. Then you allow Him to use you. When we accept that we really have no control, we can surrender and give it up to God. He knows the "before" and the "after" events of our lives. He understands what we need to learn in order to grow and change and thus become a better person. It is a combination of our experiences that builds our character. It is the pain of the suffering and hardships, the experience of struggling, and the joy of ultimate survival and success that makes us more thankful and grateful for all of our blessings and freedoms. Even though we may not understand, and it may not be obvious to us at the time, God allows things to happen for a reason and we need to trust that it is always for our best.

When we try too hard to control life's challenging events, we often mess things up. It would be wiser to hand it over to God and let our problems go. Tell yourself: "I cannot do anything about these problems, but God can, and I will trust Him to reveal the course He wants me to follow." Although it may not be easily understood, the divine power is there and it does work on your behalf when you believe—really believe—and stay relaxed in that belief. He is always ready to provide the help when we are receptive to it. If you refuse to be agitated by your problems, then His power will flow into the situation and everything that hindered a solution will melt away. You do not need to know how it will work; you just need to know that it *will* work. It is in His time and not ours. The signs of His work and the answers to our prayers are not always immediate, nor are they always what we want. It is God's will that prevails. Compte de Buffon said, "Never think that God's delays are God's denials. Hold on; hold fast; hold out. Patience is genius."(Beliefnet Daily Inspiration from Beliefnet.com, May 2004)

I believe that miracles are available to everyone, and we can make them possible by asking for them. I do not think that receiving a miracle depends on whether or not you are especially deserving. Miracles happen for everyone. "Terrible" things can and do happen to good people. A great many wonderful human beings suffer dreadful injustice and hardship. I think that God loves everyone and would help all of us without exception.

First we have to really believe, not just hope, that God can perform a miracle. Then we have to let go of the fear and place our trust in God. We need to continue to pray and leave it in his hands without restrictions and parameters. We cannot ask for it to be done by a certain date or in a certain way. We have to be open to His will.

Lessons:

Ask and you shall receive.

John 16:23

Every day presents opportunities to ask for what you want and need. These are the seeds for your future. Plant your seeds in your requests so that you can enjoy the harvest later. There is a principle that says that the world responds to those who ask. The acronym A.S.K. is helpful in remembering this: Always Seeking Knowledge.

To succeed in life, business, or personal struggle, you must always ask questions and seek the help and knowledge of others, including God. We know we can ask for what we want and that we will be heard. We must also listen for answers in our daily lives.

When others have received miracles, divine help was asked for; but it was not presumed that God would create a specific outcome. If it is God's will that someone is to die or survive, that person and his or her family have to be prepared to accept the situation and make the best of it. With God's support, things will always be alright. His comfort and love will be received regardless of the outcome.

Take a leap of faith.

Taking a leap of faith means releasing old beliefs and being open to the many different ways of viewing life and its circumstances. It might include making a change in how you see things and what you value. If you have never prayed out loud, or prayed as a family, it is hard for me to explain to you the feeling of strength and comfort that comes from it. You must experience it for yourself. I encourage you to read the scriptures and study the prayers found in this book. This is a place to start.

If you want to achieve different results, you need to do things differently. If you want changes in your life, you need to make changes in yourself. In spite of what may seem to be the impossible, you have to take the leap of faith, see clearly what you want, and believe that it can become a reality.

There are in the end three things that last, Faith, hope and Love, and the greatest of these is Love.

1 Corinthians 13:13

It was through our faith in God, our hope in the impossible, and our unconditional, overwhelming love within our family that we were able to overcome the pressures and negative forces. Mother Teresa is often quoted for saying, "We can do no great things, only small things with great love." Often when events seem overpowering, you can move ahead if you take one small step at a time.

Surround yourself with those you love.

We need not be alone in our life's challenges. There is prayer. Family, friends, neighbours, co-workers, patients, church members all over the world, from many different denominations, the Sisters in the convents, and many more were willing to help and prayed for us. It is though the combined focused efforts of many that a miracle can take place.

Focus on the positive.

When life is overwhelming and the situation seems impossible, choose to remain positive. Instead of focusing on the illness, focus on the healing. Instead of focusing on the problems, focus on the solutions. Look for the good moments and the small successes.

Remember that there is always some good that can come from every situation; there is always a lesson to be learned. You must realize how powerful your thoughts are. Since we create through thought, you should never think a defeatist or negative thought. You need to focus and concentrate on positive thoughts for your success.

During some of the low moments, when we prayed for Steven, one of the Sisters of St. Joseph who was praying for Steven said to me: "Although it is not obvious now, in the years to come you will know the purpose of this event." I held on to that thought. I watched for the lessons to be learned and, as our prayers were answered, I knew that I had to share them.

Be consistent in your prayers and belief.

I believe that we should share our life with God on a daily basis. We should not just turn to Him in our hour of need. Through prayer, we can learn to trust: all we need to do is put our best energy into our days and listen for the answers within our daily life. Know that through prayer you can share your hopes and dreams; you can ask for guidance, clarify your visions; and pray for strength and comfort. Remember to pray in gratitude for what you have and for what you believe. In *Faith, Hope and Love: An Inspirational Treasury of Quotations* (see recommended readings) the author writes, "A single grateful thought raised to heaven is the most perfect prayer."

St. Augustine, an early Christian theologian said, "Faith is to believe, on the word of God, what we do not see, and its reward is to see and enjoy what we believe." In spite of the outcome, hold on to your belief; cease the struggle to have your life follow your will. Allow yourself to be part of a divine plan; We may not see the whole plan, nor understand the reasons, but we must trust that God *does* have a divine plan. May you trust God and believe that you are exactly where you are meant to be.

When we are in emotional or physical pain, we can give it all to Him; we can surrender control to Him. Steven put his pain into his earthly father's hand; we can put ourselves into our heavenly Father's hand.

Make a battle plan.

When faced with a crisis, you need to plan how you will attack the situation and get through it. We treated the tumours as a battle. We even involved Steven in the fight. Our plan was to surround him with positive energy, humour, and love. We prayed, we asked for prayer, and we made our battle public. Unfortunately, people will pray and sit back and expect God to do all the work. You must actively do your part, asking for His guidance along the way.

You need to think differently, "outside of the box." Just because there is a popular opinion or thought does not make it the only opinion or thought. Just because the experts have an opinion does not necessarily make it the right one. Remember that medicine and traditional methods of healing as we know it in North America can only go so far. Look beyond, at every possibility, and do not be afraid to pray to God for guidance.

No one has the right to take away someone's hope.

I believe that hope is as important as any medication or treatment. To hope under the most extreme and dire circumstances is an act of defiance; it is part of the human spirit to endure and to give a miracle a chance to happen. Hope is as vital to our lives as the very oxygen we breathe. Hope is optimistic; it is a thought that things will improve, that circumstances will not always be so bleak, a way to rise above the present circumstances, or the high road where you have expectancy in your heart. Hope is an attitude of gratitude for what you believe can be; it is a positive thought, a vision of what is needed.

Without hope there is despair, and we all know that we are

going nowhere fast in that state of mind. It is impossible for hope and despair to exist simultaneously. One simply cancels the other out. Often it is despair that cancels out hope such as in the line from the prayer of St. Francis of Assisi: "Lord, make me an instrument of your peace...Where there is despair, hope." With a vision of hope we ask for the strength to cancel despair.

There are many who will try to dissuade you from your convictions. They will try to make you face their "reality." They will not understand your faith or your steadfast trust. If you have never seen or experienced the power of God before, you need to reach out to those who do believe and those who have true personal stories to share. You can borrow your belief from them, until such time as you experience His love and His power in your own life;then you will have your own faith to share with others. Once it happens, you will know what you know. Then there is an overwhelming knowing and an openness to share it with others. When people ask me, "Why are you telling this story?" I have to respond, "I have a responsibility to share it." I personally believe that once something like this happens you owe it to God, to speak in gratitude for His gift. We are telling the story for His glory. There are many other stories to be told and to be heard.

◊ ◊ ◊

Written on the cover of *Time Magazine* (April 10, 1995. Vol. 145. No. 14, 38-45), is "Can We Still Believe In Miracles?" In an article titled "The Message of Miracles," Nancy Gibbs writes of a woman whose teenaged daughter was hit by a car while rollerblading down a street. The doctors told the mother that there was no hope; the best prognosis they could offer was that her daughter would be able to feed herself some day. The family engaged very seriously, in prayer as did their Church and the Sunday school. Two weeks later the girl woke up. She is now back at school as a healthy student. In retelling this story to Gibbs, Dan Wakefield, a theological investigator, stressed that "these people were not kooks," they only spoke to the reporter because their minister asked them to do so. I know that just like in our story, there are many more stories out there that support the power of prayer and the strength of faith.

◊ ◊ ◊

My husband and I were out for a drive one evening when we happened upon a pedestrian who had just been hit by a car. The sixteen-year-old girl had just stepped off the sidewalk and into the path of a fast-moving car. She was thrown several feet by the impact and lay unconscious, cyanotic, and in critical condition when Richard got to her side. He gave her First Aid, the ABCs of CPR, and stabilized her the best he could before the paramedics arrived. When he went to the hospital later that night to see how she was, he told the family what had happened. The young girl had a severe head injury and was not expected to live. Many prayed for her. Her mother called Richard many months later to tell him that her daughter had awakened from her coma after four-and-a-half months. You cannot lose hope!

◊ ◊ ◊

You must never take away someone's hope. Always give people some hope. There is always the chance that things are not as they appear. There are unexplained events, there are miracles, and there is the power of prayer. No one person can accurately determine the final outcome 100 percent of the time.

You must not lose hope; otherwise, you cave in and lose your strength to deal with life's challenges. We all have challenges; they are part of life. Hold tight to your convictions, especially if you have faith, hope, and trust in the power of your own belief in something beyond this world.

Humour is an important part of healing.
Laughter is one of the best things that God has given us. With hearty laughter we begin to heal. Laughter has been proven to heal the body, soothe the soul, lift the spirit, and give you energy. St. Ignatius of Loyola said, "Laugh and grow strong."

Keep the Faith Beyond the Crisis

During this experience, God was at the forefront of our lives. We were so close to the Lord at that time that we have since prayed that we stay as close to him now that a considerable amount of time has passed since Steven's recovery.

Unfortunately, when time passes, it is human nature for people to go about their business, just living, and be busy with family activities and their children. It is too easy to move away from God and prayer at those times. But it is important to maintain your faith, to spread the word to others, and share your gratitude. If you can read scriptures, spiritual books, or just meditate for fifteen minutes in the morning or at night, you will gain balance and strength for what you may need to deal with daily.

During life's challenges, make a conscious effort to see the blessing. I know that when you are in the midst of a challenge, it is very hard to stand back and find the lesson or blessing in that distressful time. But if you do make the effort and successfully see the lesson, the true meaning of the challenge will appear and you will experience personal growth.

When looking back on events that were traumatic, you can see that they often served as valuable learning experiences. When you see things in this light, your insight turns to valuing the experience because it brings you to a higher, happier place in your life. It is a place of wisdom and maturity. You become a better person, or your family is stronger as a direct result of the despairing time.

The things we consider difficulties are often God's opportunities for our greater blessing. We must trust, believe, hope, and continue to walk the path He has laid before us.

It is in the writing of this book that our entire family has been blessed again by revisiting this miraculous time in our lives. We have renewed our closeness to the Lord, and our gratefulness to Him. I strongly encourage you to remember in thoughts and in prayers of gratitude the blessings of your life.

Karen's Reflections & Lessons Learned

ur Resources

CHAPTER FOURTEEN

Cards and Letters

We received cards and letters of love from people all over North America. Most of these people we had never met, but their support was appreciated. The power these cards held and the support they offered, in how they strengthened and lifted us, cannot be emphasized enough. Just knowing that the thoughts and prayers by others were with us helped get us through each and every day. Thank you to all of you. The words were inspiring and thoughts encouraging.

Dear Karen and Rick;

The Sisters of St. Joseph want you to know that they are imploring our Heavenly Father for a return to full health of your dear son, Steven. Sister St. Brigid is especially faithful to this need. You are being carried in our hearts during this most difficult time. The truth of the meaning of your suffering will be made clear sometime in the future.
God Bless You,
Sister Ann Marshall

From the Sisters of the Precious Blood Monastery
Dear Dr. and Mrs. Zizzo;

I know that half the city must be joining you and your family in prayer at this time. We would like to assure you of our prayer as well. Two phone calls were received just prior to the surgery the

other evening. And, as it so happened, the Community was in chapel praying for Steven at the time of the surgery. That day was the feast of Canada's Blessed Brother Andre. We told him that if he wanted the chance of a first-class miracle for his canonization, this was it! One never knows....We continue to pray for Steven as well as for yourselves. May Our Lady who knows so well the pain and anguish of suffering with her Son, grant you all the strength, support, courage, and faith that you need at this time.
Sincerely,
Sister Rose Marie and Sisters of the Precious Blood

Dear Dr. Richard and Family,

I just want you to know how much I am with you in prayer and concern at this time. May God restore little Steven to full health and give all of you peace and courage. His ways are mysterious at times...but He is a God of love and can bring unexpected good out of anything.
With prayerful remembrance,
Sister Linda Thompson

◊ ◊ ◊

We received so many wonderful messages full of love that I can not possibly include all of them here. But, the following ones might touch and comfort you.

One women shared a message that appeared in her church bulletin. It helped her, and she thought the words might comfort us, too.

No matter what we will have to face in life,
Hold on to the truth that Jesus Christ remains with us
And will stand with us forever.

Another card had a prayer meant to encourage:
God help you to endure and place your trust in times like these, in Him whose help is sure.

Our Resources

A personally written note read as follows:
Dear Dr. Rick,

This is just a little note to let you know that we have been thinking about you and your family during what must be a difficult and trying time for everyone. Why do bad things happen to the best people? It just doesn't seem fair. We hope there are happier days in the near future for you and Karen, and especially for your son Steven.

Of the many cards that Steven received personally, there were humorous ones, religious ones, computerized ones, and hand-drawn ones. There were some that had activities to keep him busy and some that made him laugh. He cherished all of them and keeps them to this day.

Here is a religious one:
We know God warmly cares about all creatures great and small.
That we are all His children and He watches over all.
So while you are getting better, just remember God above
Is there with you, to care for you, with tenderness and love.

Another card had this message:
All of us bought this and all of us signed it,
And we put all the strength of our wishes behind it.
'Cause all of us like you and miss you lots too
And will really be glad when you're feeling like new.

Here is a cute one:
Some get-well wishes from the heart —'cause that's where all good wishes start.
Have a good day, get lots of rest and get well soon.

After Steven's recovery Sister Mary Austin sent this note:

Dear Steven,

May you receive many blessings from Jesus as you have Him come into your heart and soul. We all know He loves you in a very special way when He brought you through such a sickness recently. I will continue to keep you in my prayers daily and hope you will say a prayer for me once in a while. May Jesus, Mary and Joseph bless and love you abundantly.
My love and prayers,
Sister Mary Austin.

To this day I cannot part with the letters and cards that we received. They all meant so much to us then, and still do. They represented the love, support, and prayers that were given so abundantly in our time of need. They showed us how many people were with us in our struggle. Knowing the power of these letters, cards, and heartfelt sentiments, I now always try to send words of encouragement to others. It is such a simple thing to write a note, or send a card, but those notes and cards allow people to know that others truly care. And it is the "knowing" that gets them through each day.

Our Resources

CHAPTER FIFTEEN

 rayers and Scriptures

The power of prayer has been recognized and practised by billions of people for thousands of years. Through prayer, people seek the guidance of a higher power for such things as health, wealth, happiness, success, world peace, and forgiveness. People pray for themselves, their families, their church congregations, and the world.

I would like to share some of the readings and prayers that came to me during our time of need. There were many times that I felt guided toward a certain scripture which always seemed to give me peace, comfort, and hope when I most needed them.

As I mentioned previously, I was led to a scripture in the Bible when I was earnestly seeking answers that first night. We had been given the serious news about Steven and we were devastated.

The scripture the Bible opened to was John 16:23.

I am telling you the truth: The Father will give you whatever you ask of him in my name. Ask and you shall receive so that your happiness may be complete.

From that moment forward, I held on to those words. I believed the words with all my heart, then I knew that I could go to the Father and ask for strength, help, guidance, and a miracle.

It is my sincere wish that these prayers and scriptures will help you too. In a moment of prayer, give your problem over to God, knowing that he is your silent, senior partner. Put the problem in His hands and say, "I am entrusting this to You." It is by far much better than trying to do it all yourself. You are asking for divine intervention, and you are symbolically taking God's hand. "Ask and you shall receive" and you will bring hope to your situation.

There is Always a Special Road for Everyone's Journey.

When God is our companion,

As we walk the road of life,

There is help for every problem

And grace for care and strife!

And we'll find that we've been happy

All along the path we've trod,

When in faith we've made the journey,

Hand in hand, along with God!

Gilbert
A Healing Love by Father Ralph Di Orio, page 143

Prayers

Prayer is answered through the zeal and endeavor we put into it. Prayer is a wonderful help, for it is the only way of really helping yourself. We can not always control the situation, but we can control our belief in prayer. There is a simple rule to follow in life. "Don't worry about anything, pray about everything."

Prayer of St. Francis of Assisi

Lord, make me an instrument of thy piece.

Where there is hatred, let me sow love.

Where there is injury, pardon.

Where there is doubt, faith.

Where there is despair, hope.

Where there is darkness, light.

Where there is sadness, joy.

Oh Divine Master, grant that I may not so much seek

To be consoled, as to console,

To be understood, as to understand,

To be loved, as to love

For it is in giving that we receive,

It is in pardoning that we are pardoned.

It is in dying to self, that we are born to eternal life.

The Power of Prayer

The day was long, the burden I had borne

Seemed heavier than I could longer bear.

And then it lifted, but I did not know

Someone had knelt in prayer.

(continued on page 126)

Prayers and Scriptures

Had taken me to God that very hour,

And asked the easing of the load, and He,

In infinite compassion, had stooped down

And taken it from me.

We cannot tell how often as we pray

For some bewildered one, hurt and distressed

The answer comes, but many times those hearts

Find sudden peace and rest.

Someone had prayed, and Faith, a reaching hand,

Took hold of God, and brought Him down that day!

So many, many hearts have need of prayer

Oh, let us pray.

From the Order of the Sisters of the Precious Blood

The Serenity Prayer

God grant me the serenity to
accept the things I cannot change
Courage to change the things I can
and the Wisdom to know the difference.

Reinhold Niebuhr

Our Resources

Our Prayers

The following prayers are in my own words. These are similar to the ones I used.

Putting Yourself in God's Hands

Dear Lord, I place myself and my loved ones in Your hands. I believe I am now receiving all of the strength and support that I will need. I feel it flowing into me. I trust that You will guide me in the direction of what is best. You know the before and the after. Your will be done.

Asking for the Lesson

Dear Lord, teach me the lesson quickly so that this burden may be lifted. Have me see what You would have me see in order for my growth. I put my faith and trust in you.

Before surgery

Dear Lord, please guide the surgeon's hands. Hold my loved one in Your hands and surround them all with Your healing power and light. I trust in You. You are the all powerful healer and will work through the physicians for our good. I know that You know best and, whatever the outcome, continue to hold our hands and walk with us. I pray that You will give strength and healing to [name of patient].

For Strength

Dear Lord, give me the strength and courage to walk this walk. Please hold my hand and stay by my side. Give me understanding and let me see the path that You have chosen so that I might have peace. Keep me strong and help me do whatever it is that You wish me to do. Help me accept that Thy will be done.

A Prayer Of Gratitude

Dear Lord, thank You for the many blessings that You have given us; our loving family and good health, our abilities and gifts, food and shelter, and the beautiful world we live in. May we be always grateful and remember to show our love to each other and to You. Thank you Lord for Your constant, unconditional love and support.

A Prayer For Healing

Thank You for the gift of our son and for the seven years we have been privileged to have had him.
Dear God, please heal our son. Save his life.
If he is not to live, please Lord, stay with us and hold our hands.
Be with us and guide us, and show us what this is all about.
We will not blame or forsake You.
We need You and we ask for You to be with us constantly.
We will find some good in this. And that is a hard thing to do.
But it is the right thing to do.
Above all, Thy will be done.

A Prayer for Protection

This is a child of God,
I will not allow any forces other than those of the Lord to be around my son.
Jesus, please surround Steven with your love, your light, and your healing.
Keep away any evil forces.
God, protect my child with your loving grace.
Above all, Thy will be done.

Our Resources

Our Hymns

"On Eagle's Wings." Tune: Michael Joncas, New Dawn Music (from Gather Comprehensive Hymnal, pages 611-612, GIA Publications, Inc., Chicago, 1994). Text from Psalm 91.

You who dwell in the shelter of the Lord, who abide in His Shadow for life, say to the Lord: "My refuge, my rock in whom I trust!"

And He shall raise you up on eagle's wings, bear you on the breath of dawn,
Make you to shine like the sun, and hold you in the palm of His hand.

The snare of the fowler will never capture you, and famine will bring you no fear:
Under His wings your refuge, his faithfulness your shield.

And He shall raise you up on eagle's wings, bear you on the breath of dawn,
Make you to shine like the sun, and hold you in the palm of His hand.

You need not fear the terror of the night, nor the arrow that flies by day;
Though thousands fall about you, near you it shall not come.

And He shall raise you up on eagle's wings, bear you on the breath of dawn,
Make you to shine like the sun, and hold you in the palm of His hand.

For to His angels He's given a command to guard you in all of your ways;
Upon their hands they will bear you up, lest you dash your foot against a stone.

And He shall raise you up on eagle's wings, bear you on the
breath of dawn,
Make you to shine like the sun, and hold you in the palm of His
hand.

"Be Not Afraid." Tune by Bob Dufford, SJ, New Dawn
Music, (from Gather Comprehensive Hymnal, pages 608-609,
GIA Publications, Inc., Chicago, 1994). Text from Isaiah 43:2-3

You shall cross the barren desert, but you shall not die of thirst.
You shall wander far in safety though you do not know the way.
You shall speak your words in foreign lands and all will understand.
You shall see the face of God and live.

Be not afraid. I go before you always. Come, follow Me, and I
will give you rest.

If you pass through raging waters in the sea, you shall not
drown.
If you walk amid the burning flames, you shall not be harmed.
If you stand before the power of hell and death is at your side,
Know that I am with you through it all.

Be not afraid. I go before you always. Come, follow Me, and I
will give you rest.

Blessed are your poor, for the kingdom shall be theirs.
Blest are you that weep and mourn, for one day you shall laugh.
And if wicked tongues insult and hate you all because of Me,
blessed, blessed are you!

Be not afraid. I go before you always. Come, follow Me, and I
will give you rest.

"Daily Prayers for Busy People." William J. O'Malley, SJ St. Mary's Press, Christian Brothers Publications, Winona, Minnesota 1990. Page 110.

How wonderful are your gifts to me;

How good you are!

You have shown me the landmarks,

My guide, my teacher, my friend.

With You at my side, I cannot fail.

So my heart and soul exult.

I stride on confidently.

You have only to point out the path.

Adapted from Psalm 16

Our Scriptures

God released His faith in words. Man is created in the image of God, therefore man released his faith in words. Words are the most powerful things in the universe today. The Word of God conceived in the human spirit, formed by the tongue, and spoken out of the mouth, becomes creative power that will work for you.

He gave them power…to heal all manner of sickness and disease.
Mathew 10:1

I received the Spirit of wisdom and revelation in the knowledge of Him, the eyes of my understanding being enlightened. And I am not conformed to this world, but I am transformed by the renewing of my mind. My mind is renewed by the Word of God
Ephesians 1:17-18 and Romans 12:2

If two of you shall agree on earth as touching anything that they shall ask, it shall be done for them of my Father which is in heaven. Where two or three are gathered together in my name, there am I, in the midst of them.
Mathew 18:19-20

May the God of hope fill you with all joy and peace, as you trust in Him, so that you may overflow with hope by the power of the Holy Spirit.
Romans 15:13

According to your faith be it unto you.
Mathew 9:29

What things you desire, when you pray, believe that you receive them, and you shall have them.
Mark 11:24

Those who hope in the Lord will renew their strength. They will soar on wings like eagles; they will run and not grow weary, they will walk and not be faint.
Isaiah 40:31

Be strong and courageous. Do not be terrified; do not be discouraged, for the Lord your God will be with you wherever you go.
Joshua 1:9

Do not fear, for I am with you; do not be dismayed, for I am your God. I will strengthen you and help you; I will uphold you with My righteous right hand.
Isaiah 41:10

Oh Lord, you are our Father. We are the clay, You are the potter; we are all the work of Your hand.
Isaiah 64:8

Show me your ways, oh Lord, teach me Your paths; guide me in Your truth and teach me, for You are God my Savior, and my hope is in You all day long.
Psalm 25:4-5

Your word is a lamp to my feet and a light for my path.
Psalm 119:105

We live by faith, not by sight.
II Corinthians 5:7

Prayers and Scriptures

Poems

Footprints

One night a man had a dream. He dreamed he was walking along the beach with the LORD. Across the sky flashed scenes from his life. For each scene, he noticed two sets of footprints in the sand: One belonged to him, and the other to the LORD.

When the last scene of his life flashed before him, he looked back at the footprints in the sand. He noticed that many times along the path of his life there was only one set of footprints. He also noticed that it happened at the very lowest and saddest times in his life.

This really bothered him and he questioned the LORD about it.

"LORD, you said that once I decided to follow you, you'd walk with me all the way. But I have noticed that during the most troublesome times in my life, there is only one set of footprints. I don't understand why when I needed you most you would leave me."

The LORD replied, "My precious, precious child, I love you and I would never leave you. During your times of trial and suffering, when you see only one set of footprints, it was then that I carried you."

Margaret Fishback Powers, 1964.

From inspirational plaques …

If God brings me to it, He will bring me through it.

The will of God will never lead you where the grace of God cannot keep you.

*L*et Go and Let God

When you are troubled and worried and sick at heart

And your plans are upset and your world falls apart

Remember God's ready and waiting to share

The burden you find much too heavy to bear.

So with faith, let go and let God, lead the way

Into a brighter and less troubled day.

Helen Steiner Rice

RECOMMENDED READING

Canfield, Jack, Mark Victor Hansen, and Les Hewitt. *The Power of Focus*. Deerfield Beach, FL: Health Communications Inc., 2000.

Chopra, Deepak, M.D. Quantum Healing: *Exploring the Frontiers of Mind/Body Medicine*. New York: Bantam Books, 1990.

Di Orio, Father Ralph A. *Healing Love*. New York: Doubleday, 1988.

Di Orio, Father Ralph A. *The Healing Power of Affirmation: Accepting God and Goodness in Your Life*. New York, NY: Doubleday, 1966.

Dossey, Larry, M.D. Healing Words, *The Power of Prayer and the Practice of Medicine*. San Francisco: Harper Collins Publishers, 1993.

Dossey, Larry, M.D. *Prayer is Good Medicine*. San Francisco: Harper Collins Publishers, 1996.

Dyer, Wayne W., PhD. *There is a Spiritual Solution to Every Problem*. New York: Quill, 2003.

Faith, Hope and Love: An Inspirational Treasury of Quotations. Philadelphia: Running Press, 1994.

Gibbs, Nancy. "The Message of Miracles." *Time Magazine*. April 10,1995. Vol. 145, No.14, 38-45.

Harpur, Tom. Prayer, *The Hidden Fire*. Kelowna, B.C.: Northstone Publishing, 1998.

Harpur, Tom. *The Uncommon Touch: An Investigation of Spiritual Healing*. Toronto: McClelland & Stewart, 1994.

Miller, Carolyn, PhD., *Creating Miracles: Understanding the Experience of Divine Intervention.* H.J. Kramer Inc., 1995.

Moon, Jannell. *How to Pray Without Being Religious: Finding Your Own Spiritual Path.* London: Element. 2004.

Myss, Caroline, PhD. *Anatomy of the Spirit: The Seven Stages of Power and Healing.* New York: Three River's Press, 1996.

Peale, Norman Vincent. *The Power of Positive Thinking.* New York: Fawcett Crest, 1982.

Powers, Margaret Fishback. *Footprints: The True Story Behind the Poem that Inspired Millions.* Toronto: Harper Collins Publishers, 1993.

Rice, Helen Steiner. *Poems of Faith.* Littlebrook Publishing Inc., 1981.

Siegel, Bernie, M.D. *Love, Medicine and Miracles.* New York: Harper Collins Publishers, 1991.

Siegel, Bernie, M.D. *Peace, Love and Healing.* New York: Quill, 2001.

Solwak, Dale. *The Power of Prayer.* Novato, CA: New World Library, 1998.

Wallace, Claudia. "Faith and Healing." *Time Magazine.* June 24, 1996. Vol. 147, No.26, 34-40.

Wilkinson, Darlene. *The Prayer of Jabez for Women: Breaking Through to the Blessed Life.* Sisters, OR: Multnomah Publishers, 2002.

Williamson, Marianne. *A Return to Love: Reflections on the Principles of a Course in Miracles.* New York: Harper Collins Publishers, 1992.

Recommended Reading

AUTHOR'S POSTSCRIPT

If you would care to share your personal stories, miracles, or divine interventions with me, I would appreciate hearing about them and could possibly include them in a future book. I can be reached at the following address:

Enlighten Publishing
27 Legend Court, P.O. Box 10114
Ancaster, Ontario
Canada
L9K 1P3

About The Author

Karen Zizzo has a Master of Arts Degree in Sociology from McMaster University, in Hamilton, Ontario. She taught at Mohawk College for ten years; ran her own retail business, "The Children's Garden of Westdale" for nine years; and was a small-business consultant and corporate trainer for six years. She currently builds an on-line e-commerce business network.

Karen is an author, publisher, and professional speaker with a passion for inspiring people to overcome the obstacles in their lives. Through her keynote speeches she generously shares a very personal message of hope.

Karen is the mother of three grown children: Steven, Laura, and Ryan. She has been married to her husband, Richard, a physician, for thirty years. They reside in Ancaster, Ontario, Canada.

Our Resources

$\mathcal{S}$ignificance of the Cover Photo

Steven arrived at Tamarama Beach, New South Wales, Australia at 5 a.m. to take this picture.

For our family, the sunrise represents Hope; the water represents the flow and ebb of Life; the one set of unknown footprints in the sand signifies God carrying us.

When Steven left after taking this photo, he turned and saw a fisherman down the beach. This fisherman had not been present moments earlier when Steven arrived.

Prayers and Scriptures

BIBLICAL REFERNCES

Scriptures in this book have been taken from the following Bibles:

The Catholic Living Bible. Wheaton, IL: Tyndale House Publishers, 1976.

The Holy Bible: New International Version (North America). International Bible Society, 1984.

The Living Bible. Wheaton, IL: Tyndale House Publishers, 1972.

The New American Bible. Wichita, KS: Catholic Bible Publishers, 1973.

Notes:

I will not forget you.
I have held you
in the palm of my hand.

Isaiah 49:15-16

Waking up to what is already present